بسم ،لله الرحمن الرحيم

All translations from the Qur'an are from
"The Noble Qur'an: a New Rendering of its Meaning in English"
by Hajj Abdalhaqq and Aisha Bewley,
published by Bookwork, Norwich, UK. 1420 CE/1999 AH

By Harun Yahya

Edited By: Abdassamad Clarke

ISBN 1842000 42x
Printed and bound by:
San Ofset
Cendere Yolu No:23 Ayazaga/Istanbul
Tel: 0212 289 24 24 (pbx)

Website:
http://www.hyahya.org
http://www.harunyahya.com
E-mail: info@harunyahya.com

THE WORLD OF ANIMALS

HARUN YAHYA

About The Author

The author, who writes under the pen-name HARUN YAHYA, was born in Ankara in 1956. Having completed his primary and secondary education in Ankara, he then studied arts at Istanbul's Mimar Sinan University and philosophy at Istanbul University. Since the 1980s, the author has published many books on political, faith-related and scientific issues. Harun Yahya is well-known as an author who has written very important works disclosing the imposture of evolutionists, the invalidity of their claims and the dark liaisons between Darwinism and bloody ideologies such as fascism and communism.

His pen-name is made up of the names "Harun" (Aaron) and "Yahya" (John), in memory of the two esteemed prophets who fought against lack of faith. The Prophet's seal on the cover of the author's books has a symbolic meaning linked to the their contents. This seal represents the Qur'an, the last Book and the last word of Allah, and our Prophet, the last of all the prophets. Under the guidance of the Qur'an and Sunnah, the author makes it his main goal to disprove each one of the fundamental tenets of godless ideologies and to have the "last word", so as to completely silence the objections raised against religion. The seal of the Prophet, who attained ultimate wisdom and moral perfection, is used as a sign of his intention of saying this last word.

All these works by the author centre around one goal: to convey the message of the Qur'an to people, thus encouraging them to think about basic faith-related issues, such as the existence of Allah, His unity and the hereafter, and to display the decrepit foundations and perverted works of godless systems.

Harun Yahya enjoys a wide readership in many countries, from India to America, England to Indonesia, Poland to Bosnia, and Spain to Brazil. Some of his books are available in English, French, German, Italian, Spanish, Portuguese, Urdu, Arabic, Albanian, Russian, Serbo-Croat (Bosnian), Polish, Malay, Uygur Turkish, and Indonesian, and they have been enjoyed by readers all over the world.

Greatly appreciated all around the world, these works have been instrumental in many people putting their faith in Allah and in many others gaining a deeper insight into their faith. The wisdom, and the sincere and easy-to-understand style employed give these books a distinct touch which directly strikes any one who reads or examines them. Immune to objections, these works are characterised by their features of rapid effectiveness, definite results and irrefutability. It is unlikely that those who read these books and give a serious thought to them can any longer sincerely advocate the materialistic philosophy, atheism and any other perverted ideology or philosophy. Even if they continue to advocate, this will be only a sentimental insistence since these books have refuted these ideologies from their very basis. All contemporary movements of denial are ideologically defeated today, thanks to the collection of books written by Harun Yahya.

There is no doubt that these features result from the wisdom and lucidity of the Qur'an. The author certainly does not feel proud of himself; he merely intends to serve as a means in one's search for Allah's right path. Furthermore, no material gain is sought in the publication of these works.

Considering these facts, those who encourage people to read these books, which open the "eyes" of the heart and guide them in becoming more devoted servants of Allah, render an invaluable service.

Meanwhile, it would just be a waste of time and energy to propagate other books which create confusion in peoples' minds, lead man into ideological chaos, and which, clearly have no strong and precise effects in removing the doubts in peoples' hearts, as also verified from previous experience. It is apparent that it is impossible for books devised to emphasize the author's literary power rather than the noble goal of saving people from loss of faith, to have such a great effect. Those who doubt this can readily see that the sole aim of Harun Yahya's books is to overcome disbelief and to disseminate the moral values of the Qur'an. The success, impact and sincerity this service has attained are manifest in the reader's conviction.

One point needs to be kept in mind: The main reason for the continuing cruelty and conflict, and all the ordeals the majority of people undergo is the ideological prevalence of disbelief. These things can only come to an end with the ideological defeat of disbelief and by ensuring that everybody knows about the wonders of creation and Qur'anic morality, so that people can live by it. Considering the state of the world today, which forces people into the downward spiral of violence, corruption and conflict, it is clear that this service has to be provided more speedily and effectively. Otherwise, it may be too late.

It is no exaggeration to say that the collection of books by Harun Yahya have assumed this leading role. By the Will of Allah, these books will be the means through which people in the 21st century will attain the peace and bliss, justice and happiness promised in the Qur'an.

The works of the author include *The New Masonic Order, Judaism and Freemasonry, Global Freemasonry, Islam Denounces Terrorism, Terrorism: The Devil's Ritual, The Disasters Darwinism Brought to Humanity, Communism in Ambush, Fascism: The Bloody Ideology of Darwinism, The 'Secret Hand' in Bosnia, Behind the Scenes of The Holocaust, Behind the Scenes of Terrorism, Israel's Kurdish Card, The Oppression Policy of Communist China and Eastern Turkestan, Palestine, Solution: The Values of the Qur'an, The Winter of Islam and Its Expected Spring, Articles 1-2-3, A Weapon of Satan: Romantism, Signs from the Chapter of the Cave to the Last Times, Signs of the Last Day, The Last Times and The Beast of the Earth, Truths 1-2, The Western World Turns to Allah, The Evolution Deceit, Precise Answers to Evolutionists, The Blunders of Evolutionists, Confessions of Evolutionists, The Qur'an Denies Darwinism, Perished Nations, For Men of Understanding, The Prophet Moses, The Prophet Joseph, The Prophet Mohammed, The Prophet Solomon, The Golden Age, Allah's Artistry in Colour, Glory is Everywhere, The Importance of the Evidences of Creation, The Truth of the Life of This World, The Nightmare of Disbelief, Knowing the Truth, Eternity Has Already Begun, Timelessness and the Reality of Fate, Matter: Another Name for Illusion, The Little Man in the Tower, Islam and the Philosophy of Karma, The Dark Magic of Darwinism, The Religion of Darwinism, The Collapse of the Theory of Evolution in 20 Questions, Allah is Known Through Reason, The Qur'an Leads the Way to Science, The Real Origin of Life, Consciousness in the Cell, A String of Miracles, The Creation of the Universe, Miracles of the Qur'an, The Design in Nature, Self-Sacrifice and Intelligent Behaviour Models in Animals, The End of Darwinism, Deep Thinking, Never Plead Ignorance, The Green Miracle: Photosynthesis, The Miracle in the Cell, The Miracle in the Eye, The Miracle in the Spider, The Miracle in the Gnat, The Miracle in the Ant, The Miracle of the Immune System, The Miracle of Creation in Plants, The Miracle in the Atom, The Miracle in the Honeybee, The Miracle of Seed, The Miracle of Hormone, The Miracle of the Termite, The Miracle of the Human Body, The Miracle of Man's Creation, The Miracle of Protein, The Miracle of Smell and Taste, The Secrets of DNA.*

The author's childrens books are: *Wonders of Allah's Creation, The World of Animals, The Splendour in the Skies, Wonderful Creatures, Let's Learn Our Religion, The World of Our Little Friends: The Ants, Honeybees That Build Perfect Combs, Skillful Dam Builders: Beavers.*

The author's other works on Quranic topics include: *The Basic Concepts in the Qur'an, The Moral Values of the Qur'an, Quick Grasp of Faith 1-2-3, Ever Thought About the Truth?, Crude Understanding of Disbelief, Devoted to Allah, Abandoning the Society of Ignorance, The Real Home of Believers: Paradise, Knowledge of the Qur'an, Qur'an Index, Emigrating for the Cause of Allah, The Character of the Hypocrite in the Qur'an, The Secrets of the Hypocrite, The Names of Allah, Communicating the Message and Disputing in the Qur'an, Answers from the Qur'an, Death Resurrection Hell, The Struggle of the Messengers, The Avowed Enemy of Man: Satan, The Greatest Slander: Idolatry, The Religion of the Ignorant, The Arrogance of Satan, Prayer in the Qur'an, The Theory of Evolution, The Importance of Conscience in the Qur'an, The Day of Resurrection, Never Forget, Disregarded Judgements of the Qur'an, Human Characters in the Society of Ignorance, The Importance of Patience in the Qur'an, General Information from the Qur'an, The Mature Faith, Before You Regret, Our Messengers Say, The Mercy of Believers, The Fear of Allah, Jesus Will Return, Beauties Presented by the Qur'an for Life, A Bouquet of the Beauties of Allah 1-2-3-4, The Iniquity Called "Mockery," The Mystery of the Test, The True Wisdom According to the Qur'an, The Struggle with the Religion of Irreligion, The School of Yusuf, The Alliance of the Good, Slanders Spread Against Muslims Throughout History, The Importance of Following the Good Word, Why Do You Deceive Yourself?, Islam: The Religion of Ease, Enthusiasm and Excitement in the Qur'an, Seeing Good in Everything, How do the Unwise Interpret the Qur'an?, Some Secrets of the Qur'an, The Courage of Believers, Being Hopeful in the Qur'an, Justice and Tolerance in the Qur'an, Basic Tenets of Islam, Those Who do not Listen to the Qur'an, Taking the Qur'an as a Guide, A Lurking Threat: Heedlessness, Sincerity in the Qur'an.*

To The Reader

In all the books by the author, faith-related issues are explained in the light of the Qur'anic verses and people are invited to learn Allah's words and to live by them. All the subjects that concern Allah's verses are explained in such a way as to leave no room for doubt or question marks in the reader's mind. The sincere, plain and fluent style employed ensures that everyone of every age and from every social group can easily understand the books. This effective and lucid narrative makes it possible to read them in a single sitting. Even those who rigorously reject spirituality are influenced by the facts recounted in these books and cannot refute the truthfulness of their contents.

This book and all the other works of the author can be read individually or discussed in a group at a time of conversation. Those readers who are willing to profit from the books will find discussion very useful in the sense that they will be able to relate their own reflections and experiences to one another.

In addition, it will be a great service to the religion to contribute to the presentation and reading of these books, which are written solely for the good pleasure of Allah. All the books of the author are extremely convincing. For this reason, for those who want to communicate the religion to other people, one of the most effective methods is to encourage them to read these books.

It is hoped that the reader will take time to look through the review of other books on the final pages of the book, and appreciate the rich source of material on faith-related issues, which are very useful and a pleasure to read.

In these books, you will not find, as in some other books, the personal views of the author, explanations based on dubious sources, styles that are unobservant of the respect and reverence due to sacred subjects, nor hopeless, doubt-creating, and pessimistic accounts that create deviations in the heart.

THE WORLD OF ANIMALS

HARUN YAHYA

Ta-Ha Publishers Ltd.
I Wynne Road London SW9 OBB
United Kingdom

CONTENTS

INTRODUCTION

Dear children,

In this book, we will discover the marvels of creation in the living beings surrounding us. In the following pages, you will set out on a joyful journey in the company of many loveable living beings who will amaze you with their many interesting and astonishing characteristics.

While reading this book, you will see that Allah has created all living beings in perfect forms and that all of them are only manifestations of Allah's infinite beauty, power and knowledge.

"Do you know all the animals?" We can hear you saying, "Not really. Only some of them." Do you know about these creatures' lives? Do you know how they are born? How they live? How they protect themselves and find food? You probably have no idea about most of the details of these animals' lives. But don't worry! As you read this book, you will learn astounding things about them and be amazed at the various perfections and fine qualities Allah has given these living creatures.

You are already acquainted with many animals. But in this book, you will also get to know some other animals' secret and marvellous worlds,

which you have most probably never heard about or seen. You will like them very much. As you continue reading, you will be amazed at the way these animals can accomplish some of the tasks they do. You will see ostriches–the fastest runners in the world, tigers–some of the best sprinters, sharp-teethed squirrels, eye-catching peacocks and, as you meet them, you will come to know them better. Meanwhile, keep in mind that these are only some of the animals that exist in the world... Our planet abounds with countless other animal species.

While seeing the beauties of these creatures, keep in mind that Allah, the Creator of all these creatures, only wants us to think about the infinite might and art in His creation, recognise that He has created everything and that He is the owner of every living being. He also wants us to see the beauty in these living creatures, to take pleasure from their beauty and thereby love Allah and be grateful to Him because He has created all these splendid creatures.

The creation of all the universe, all the lovely animals, plants, night and day and everything surrounding you serves a single purpose: to come to be able to see the sublime and flawless creation of Allah. The purpose is simply to make us, human beings, say, "How graciously Allah has created!" Reading The World of Animals will provide this outlook on the living creatures you see around you.

Are you ready? Now, turn the page and embark on The World of Animals! There is a whole world of wonderful animals waiting for you inside!

THE SQUIRREL: THE WALNUT-LOVER

In this section, we are going to learn about some of the very interesting qualities Allah has given squirrels. We are sure what you will read about these loveable little beings will also amaze your friends.

Squirrels live mostly in the forests of Europe and north America. They are about 25 centimetres (10 inches) long. That is the size of two of your hands. Behind them and often suspended over their backs are their tails, wide, upright and furry, and almost the same size as their length. There is surely a purpose why Allah, Who creates everything with a purpose, has given squirrels such a tail: Thanks to this long tail, a squirrel can jump from one tree to another without losing its balance.

The sharp little nails of a squirrel allow it to climb trees without difficulty. It can readily run along branches, hang upside-down and move while in this position. A grey squirrel in particular can jump from the tip of a branch

to the branch of another tree four metres (157 inches) away. While jumping, it extends its fore and hind limbs and glides. Meanwhile, its flattened tail both maintains its balance and serves as a rudder to steer it. It can even experience free-fall from a branch nine metres (354 inches) above the ground and land smoothly on the ground on four feet.

Now, let's consider once again what these loveable squirrels can accomplish. You already know that squirrels can perform gymnastic moves in the air quite easily, such as jumping from one tree to another without falling and, furthermore, target very tiny branches from a distance and skilfully hold on to them like a trapeze artist.

But how? Well, squirrels can achieve all these feats by using their hind limbs, their keen eyes, which make good adjustments for distances, their strong paws, and their tails, which enable them to maintain balance. But, have you ever thought who has given squirrels these features and taught them how to use them? Since it is impossible for a squirrel family to take a ruler and measure the heights of trees and lengths of branches, how do they measure distances as they jump from one tree to another? Furthermore, how do they jump and bounce so fast without getting hurt or crippled?

No doubt, it is Allah Who has created these animals together with the features they have and taught them how to use them. Furthermore,

squirrels possess all the necessary skills and physical attributes to reach walnuts, chestnuts, hazelnuts and pine nuts, the hard-shelled fruits that grow on top of high trees. As with all other animals in nature, Allah specially created squirrels so that they can readily attain the kind of food they need.

In wintertime it becomes hard for squirrels to find food, so in summer they gather food to eat in the long, cold months ahead. Squirrels are among those living beings that store food for winter.

However, squirrels are very careful while gathering their food. They don't store fruits and meat, the kind of food that decays quickly. If they gathered them, they would become hungry in the wintertime. For this reason, squirrels collect only durable dry fruits like walnuts, hazelnuts and cones.

It is Allah Who gives this knowledge to squirrels at birth and enables them

to take their nutrition. Here, we witness one of the attributes of Allah: Allah is "ar-Razzaq", that is, "the One Who continually provides sustenance to every living being He has created".

Squirrels store their food for winter by burying it in various places. Thanks to their perfect sense of smell, they can detect the smell of nuts covered by 30 centimetres (12 inches) of snow.

Squirrels carry their food in their sacs and take them to their nests. In their nests, there are more than one store, most of which they have forgotten. Certainly there is also a divine reason for this, because in time the dry fruits forgotten by squirrels under the earth grow into new trees.

TEETH THAT ARE RENEWED WHEN BROKEN

Squirrels have strong sharp teeth such as human beings never possess. Located at the front of their mouth are incisor teeth that enable them to gnaw and break hard substances. Located behind them are the molar teeth. When we want to break a walnut, we either use a big stone or a device especially designed for this purpose. These little animals, however, can readily accomplish this with their sharp teeth.

Have you ever wondered how squirrels' teeth stay strong throughout a lifetime and how squirrels whose teeth are broken manage to eat hazelnuts or walnuts? Allah, Who has created everything in perfect harmony, has given their teeth a very important characteristic. You will indeed be very astonished when you hear this! Even if squirrels' teeth break or wear out, new teeth grow immediately. Worn-out teeth are continually replaced by growing ones. Moreover, Allah has not only given this characteristic to squirrels but also to all creatures who have to gnaw their food.

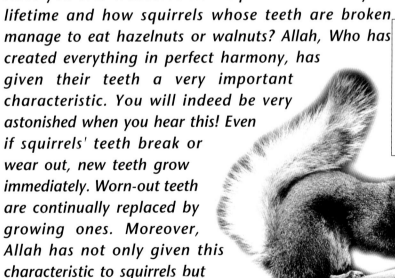

Like most other animals, squirrels do have methods of communication with one another. Red squirrels, for example, upon seeing an enemy, shake their tails and begin to make excited noises.

Squirrels, who can run on high tree branches also use their tails for balance. They change their direction by rotating their tails. The tails of squirrels serve the same function as the rudder of a vessel. The whiskers of a squirrel also play a major role in their keeping their balance. When squirrels' whiskers are cut, they cannot maintain their balance. This aside, they also use their whiskers to sense the objects around them at nights.

Children! Do you know that some squirrel species can also fly? All the "flying squirrel" species in Australia, whose heights vary from 45 to 90 centimetres (18 to 35 inches), live on trees. We cannot say that they really fly. They make long jumps from one tree to another. These creatures, who move among trees like gliders, have no wings but "flying membranes". The "sugar glider", a kind of flying squirrel with a flying membrane that extends from the fore to hind limbs, has a narrow body and long tassel-like hairs. In some species, the flying membrane is made up of furry skin. This membrane extends to the wrist of the forelimb. The gliding squirrel jumps from the trunk of a tree and can traverse about 30 metres (1181 inches) at a time by means of a glide-like effect produced by its stretched membrane. In some cases, they can even make six successive glides, covering a total distance of 530 metres (20866 inches).

When they don't move, the bodies of these small animals quickly lose

heat and they become vulnerable to freezing. For this reason, sleeping is a great threat to squirrels. However, Allah has created various protective mechanisms for every species, enabling them to survive under unfavourable environmental conditions. During sleep, for instance, squirrels just curl their fluffy tails tightly around their bodies. The tail of the squirrel is just like a coat. On wintry days, their tails save them from freezing.

RABBITS LIKE CARROTS!

Would you like to learn a bit more about rabbits, the loveable little living creatures we sometimes keep in our houses as pets? We always think of them with their snow-white fur, which we take such pleasure in stroking, and the way they gnaw carrots. Let's explore some of the interesting characteristics of these animals with which we are not familiar:

If you try to approach a rabbit, you will immediately recognise how fast it escapes. Do you know that these creatures can readily sense their enemies with their long ears even while their heads are down eating grass? Owing to this keen sense of hearing, you can hardly approach them without them noticing you. Before long, they will perceive a minor noise or movement and will run away.

Rabbits become 50 to 70 centimetres (19 to 27 inches) long when they grow into adults. Their hind limbs are longer and stronger than their forelimbs. That is why they can run 60 to 70 kilometres (37 to 43 miles) per hour and can

leap six metres forward at a time. A rabbit can move faster than a car travelling within the city does.

All rabbits possess these characteristics at birth. Allah has created them as fast runners and thus enabled them to escape their predators easily.

What do you think the answer of a rabbit would be if we were to ask it, "Which food do you like most?" Yes, you are right! He would certainly say "carrots." (Meanwhile, remember that carrots are good for our eyes.) Well, do you know that rabbits live in the warrens they dig under the ground, and that carrots grow towards the depths of the earth? As you may understand from this question, carrots have been created in the most appropriate way to meet rabbits' needs.

Also for us, human beings, Allah has made everything easy to use. Take, for instance, the orange you eat in wintertime. If it were not in segments, it would be very hard for you to eat it, because it is so juicy. However, Allah, Who has created everything you see around you, has also created this delicious fruit full of vitamin C in its segmented form, ready to eat, in its special package. Now back to rabbits! A rabbit can easily gnaw a carrot with its continually growing front teeth that give it such a lovely look.

Apart from their nutritional needs, Allah has given living creatures many features that make life easy for them. Various rabbit species with different characteristics live on earth. Rabbits living in cold regions, for example, are mostly white in colour. This is an important feature that makes them invisible on the snow and enables them to hide themselves effortlessly. Wild rabbits, which are relatively bigger than other rabbits, have longer limbs and ears. The desert American rabbit, on the other hand, has quite large ears. These ears help rabbits to keep themselves cool.

In nature, most animals live in particular territories they mark out for themselves. This is similar to us living in our comfortable homes surrounded by our family members. Animals and animal groups usually avoid entering other animals' territories. "Leaving a scent" is a method employed by animals to mark their territories. Gazelles, for instance, leave a substance with a scent similar to tar on long thin branches and grasses to mark their territory. This substance, secreted from the glands under their eyes, informs

other gazelles that this field is already occupied. Reindeer, on the other hand, have scent glands on the tip of their hind feet with which they mark their territory. Rabbits mark their territories with glands on their chins.

As we have seen, Allah has created animals with very interesting and important characteristics. Learning all these makes us astonished at the flawless creation of Allah. We remember that Allah is our Creator and we feel grateful to Him. Remember that Allah has commanded people to think about His blessings and be thankful. In a verse of the Qur'an, Allah informs us that He will reward those who are thankful:

We will recompense the thankful. (Surah Al 'Imran: 145)

Children! So, you must also remember to be thankful for the blessings and beauty with which you are surrounded.

THE LOYAL ANIMAL: THE DOG

Dogs are smarter than most creatures. They are easy to educate. Well-educated dogs are sometimes used as watchdogs. A watchdog can render a creature that is five to six times bigger ineffective. It is interesting, though, that these dogs, which can become terrifyingly wild in times of danger, pose no harm to their owners. In the face of a threat, they put their lives in jeopardy to save their owners and under no circumstances do they abandon them.

The existence of hundreds of dog species of different colours and sizes is one of the signs of Allah's matchless creation. In the Qur'an, our Lord's unique creation is related as follows:

He is the Originator of the heavens and the earth. How could He have a son when He has no wife? He created all things and He has knowledge of all things. That is Allah, your Lord. There is no god but Him, the Creator of everything. So worship Him. He is responsible for everything. (Surat al-An'am: 101-102)

Let's consider the following: assume that you have never seen a dog before and somebody asks you to draw a picture of one. Would you be

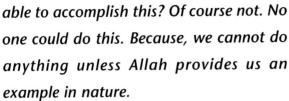

able to accomplish this? Of course not. No one could do this. Because, we cannot do anything unless Allah provides us an example in nature.

Aeroplanes, for example, are designed in imitation of the flying systems of birds. Robots are imitations of man's body systems. However, our Lord has created countless species without any previous example: Penguins living at the south pole, lions – the kings of the savannah, dolphins, butterflies, birds and bees, etc., in short, Allah created all creatures.

Allah, Who has given all creatures various features, has also given dogs physical characteristics that make them different from other living beings. For example, dogs have 42 teeth, that is, 10 more than human beings. This way, they can grind and break their food, especially bones, into pieces without difficulty. Moreover, thanks to the special creation of their eyes, in darkness dogs have better eyesight than human beings. They can perceive moving objects from farther away. Furthermore, because dogs can hear voices at frequencies beyond our threshold of hearing, they notice noises from distances four times farther away than we can. For example, a man cannot hear the extremely high-pitched sound of the dog whistle used to give commands to dogs while dogs can hear it easily.

The dog's sense of smell is also very keen. The olfactory centre – the centre for smelling – in its brain is forty times more developed than that of man. For this reason, their sense of smell is superior to man's.

By means of all these abilities, dogs can sense the smell of prey, trace it and fetch a hunter's catch even if it is kilometres away. A sniff of something belonging to a person suffices for a police dog to find its owner. Those huge flabby-cheeked dogs the Saint Bernards, for example, can easily detect injured people stuck beneath the snow with their sensitive noses and rescue them. This extraordinary sense of smell that dogs have is itself a miracle.

Dogs also use their noses to breathe air. Passing through the nose, air is filtered, warmed and moisturised and then it makes its way to the lungs.

Unlike human beings, these creatures do not sweat to regulate their body temperatures, because there are no sweat glands in their body. Regulation of body temperature is handled by the respiratory system. The hair covering the body isolates the skin from external heat. As the external temperature

increases, a dog's body temperature also increases; a dog whose body temperature increases gets rid of this excess heat by sticking out its tongue. This way, in spite of their thick hair, they do not sweat on hot days. Allah has given them such a perfect system, whereas we, human beings, immediately sweat when we run even for half an hour. But dogs never sweat even if they run for hours. Now that you have learned this fact, you don't have to worry about dogs when you see them with their tongues lolling out on hot days.

Also, if you think about dogs, you will remember that their bodies are always very soft and bright. What gives this softness and brightness to their skin is its oil glands.

There are some special systems within dogs' bodies. Thanks to these systems, the paws of a dog are never hurt, nor do they wear out and their claws never become irritated. As you see, our Lord has solved even a minor problem of one creature by means of a protective mechanism He has designed for it. Our Lord creates everything in harmony. As this example also shows, Allah has equipped all creatures with the abilities they need. Such examples lead us to think and to realise the artistry in our Lord's creation.

LITTLE WHITE LAMBS

You have most probably noticed that all lambs have tiny, cute innocent faces. There are also those bigger ones that closely resemble them. They are the mothers of the lambs, that is the ewes. Do you know that there are strong bonds between the lamb and her mother? These strong bonds are established by the time the ewes begin to feed the lambs.

By the time the ewe gives birth to her lamb, she never forgets its smell and the taste she senses while she cleans it with her tongue. That is why, she never accepts another lamb having a different taste and smell. This is really astonishing! While a mother in a hospital may well accept somebody else's

baby given to her, a ewe can readily distinguish her own lamb from all others in a crowded flock.

However, the ewe has not much time to get to know her own young one; she has to manage this as soon as she delivers the lamb. Otherwise, she could never find her lamb in a crowded flock again. Yet, she is never afflicted with such a problem, because Allah inspires her to lick her offspring as soon as she gives birth to it so that she can know its taste and smell.

Well, do you know what protects a lamb from rain? Its skin! As lambskin consists of a soft fatty layer, it serves as a raincoat preventing the lamb from becoming wet. This makes its wool curl and remain dry on rainy days.

Besides, one of the most important characteristics of lambs is their rumination. Have you ever seen an animal ruminating? Let us tell you about it. Some animals that feed on grass ruminate. Characteristically, these animals have a stomach divided into four compartments. When the animal eats something, the food first goes to the stomach then comes back to the mouth again. After the animal chews it, it goes to the other chamber of the

stomach. This process is called "rumination". Our Lord has given this capability to some animals the better to digest some indigestible foods.

Sheep and lambs have many uses for us. Every day they provide milk, and sheep milk is commonly drunk and used in many parts of the world.

The calcium in milk is essential for the development of bones and teeth. Some basic foods such as yoghurt and cheese are made of milk. Milk is also used for making cakes, pastry and other dishes. In short, milk is one of the most useful nutriments that we use everyday. Furthermore, yarns produced from their wool are used in weaving cloth for us. Yarns and threads used in many other fields have made our lives easier. In the Qur'an, which is the Book Allah has sent down to people, the uses these animals provide men are related as follows:

> **Allah has made your houses places of rest for you and made houses for you out of cattle hides which are light for you to carry both when you are travelling and when you are staying in one place. And from their wool and fur and hair you obtain clothing and carpets and household utensils for a time. (Surat an-Nahl: 80)**

> **We give you pure milk to drink, easy for drinkers to swallow. (Surat an-Nahl: 80)**

As mentioned in these verses, we benefit from sheep and lambs. We should be very grateful for these blessings that Allah has created for us.

OUR FAITHFUL FRIENDS: HORSES

Do you know that after dogs, our most loyal friends are horses? Domestic horses never leave their owners if they are able not to.

These loyal friends, which comprise more than twenty-five species, can carry us kilometres without becoming tired. Horses are the animals that have helped man most throughout history.

Today, you can see thousands of cars on the streets and there are many motorways built for these cars. Cars, however, came into the service of man only in the last century. At the time your grandfather's grandfather was born, there were no cars. In those years, animals, especially horses, were used for transportation.

Do you know that you can identify the age of a horse by looking at its incisors? Indeed, since the grass on which horses feed contains sand and dust, their teeth wear out gradually and the degree of this indicates their age. Despite this, however, horses' teeth are very long. These teeth are similar to long strips buried deep in the roots of the jawbone. That is, compared to our teeth, the roots of horses' teeth reside deep inside. As the teeth wear out,

the part remaining in the jawbone begins to emerge. In fact, the roots of the teeth of very old horses appear on the surface of the gum. Each tooth may wear out about two and a half to five centimetres (one to two inches) before it loses its ability to chew. Think for a moment: had our Lord not given this feature to horses, these animals would quickly lose their teeth and die of starvation.

Our Lord has also given another important ability to the hair of horses. Horsehair serves as a thermostat—a device used to regulate body temperature —for the animal. Their body must always remain at a constant body temperature of 38 degrees Centigrade (100.4 F). To maintain this temperature, the hair of the horse becomes longer in winter. In hot seasons, horses shed their hair, thereby maintaining this body temperature.

Here is another interesting feature of horses: Horses sleep on their feet! Do you know how they manage not to fall down? Because their leg bones have the ability to lock themselves while asleep. Thanks to this ability our Lord has given horses, they can sleep on their feet and also carry very heavy loads. The heads of human beings, however, fall down even when they fall asleep in an armchair.

Horses' legs are specially created not only to make them carry heavy loads but also to make them run very fast. Unlike other animals, horses do not have collarbones, a feature that enables them to take bigger steps. Besides, there is a bone-muscle mechanism in their limbs that, as they gain speed, decreases the amount of energy they spend and increases their ability to move. The functioning principles of this mechanism is similar to the gear mechanism in cars. Just as an accelerating car shifts to a higher gear,

horses, too, shift to a higher gear when they want to run faster. While the force required for pushing decreases, the ability to move increases.

Well, why are horses' bodies designed in a way to make them carry heavy loads and run very fast? Actually, carrying heavy loads or running very fast are not skills that a horse needs for itself. So, why do horses have these abilities?

The answer is obvious. These skills have been given to horses not to meet their own needs but to serve human beings. In other words, Allah has created horses with these abilities so that they can serve human beings. In the Qur'an, our Lord stresses that He has created animals to serve people:

And He created livestock. There is warmth for you in them, and various uses and some you eat. And there is beauty in them for you in the evening when you bring them home and in the morning when you drive them out to graze. They carry your loads to lands you would never reach except with great difficulty. Your Lord is All-Gentle, Most Merciful. And horses, mules and donkeys both to ride and for adornment. And He creates other things you do not know. (Surat an-Nahl: 5-8)

HORSES IN STRIPES: ZEBRAS

Zebras at first sight remind us of horses. As in the case of horses, zebras, too, have hair which we call a "mane". Their body structures are also very similar to horses and they run as fast as them.

Yet, their appearance is strikingly different. As you might also suppose, this difference lies in the straight stripes that cover their bodies from head to toe. Do not underestimate a stripe, since these stripes are different in every single zebra. Just like the fingerprint, which is unique to every person, the stripes of zebras are all different. Stripes provide identification data for a zebra just like an ID card does for humans. The vertical stripes of zebras are also an important element of defence. When they come together, tigers and lions perceive the herd as a whole. In this case, it becomes difficult for the predator to choose the individual zebra, which becomes a protection for the zebras.

There are two essential elements necessary for zebras to survive: water and grass.

At times, a zebra herd wanders for 50 kilometres (31 miles) to find water and grass. But at nights they return to their own places. That is because, as we mentioned earlier about other animals, each herd leads its life in a particular territory.

Do you know that zebras very much like to take dust-baths? Indeed, zebras are very fond of dust-baths. That is because, dust-baths remove the parasites living on their bodies. Apart from this, zebras have guests that accompany them and help them in their cleaning. Oxpeckers feed on the ticks found on the hides of zebras. This way, one by one they pick the parasites that make zebras sick and cause them to itch. As you see, our Lord, Who plans and controls the lives of all the creatures and makes them helpers for each other, has also assigned some animals as helpers of others.

About half an hour after birth, a new-born zebra stands up and begins to walk, though in a faltering trembling manner. No sooner do they walk than they begin to suck their mothers' milk. Milk is very beneficial for a new-born creature. This milk, which is pink in colour by a special creation of Allah, protects them from illnesses from birth onwards. Besides that, it secures the proper functioning of their intestines.

Zebras, as is the case with all other creatures under Allah's protection, are equipped with defence mechanisms that Allah has taught them. The first of these defence mechanisms is their very sensitive sensory organs, such as seeing, hearing and smell, which Allah has given them at birth. The sensitivity of these sensory organs enables zebras to notice their predators quickly and run away. No sooner do they begin to run than they reach an incredible speed. The second defence mechanism is the following: when the herd fall asleep, one or two zebras stay awake and watch out for possible threats.

Zebras employ the defence tactics that are similar to those of human beings. However, it is interesting that these animals live in harmony in herds and make a division of labour. It is obvious that it is Allah Who creates zebras, collects them together and provides their sustenance and Who commands them to make a division of labour. If this was not the case, no one would be able to explain why some zebras make sacrifices such as staying awake all night long to protect the others.

On the other hand, for the new-born zebra who has recently opened his eyes to this world, the defence tactics Allah has taught him are much simpler. All he has to do is stay close to his mother. That is because, it is impossible for a new-born zebra to see stealthy enemies with his newly opened eyes or run away from them with his weak, trembling limbs. You see, Allah has inspired the new-born zebra to remain next to his mother always until he grows up. Otherwise, how could he know that there are predators around waiting for him and that the most secure place for him is with his mother?

Most zebras live on open grasslands where there is not much possibility to hide. For this reason, in order to stay alive, they need to move very fast. All the body structure of a zebra is devised to meet this need. For instance, their limbs are very long; they can run very long distances without becoming exhausted or losing speed. Although light, the bones of zebras are very strong.

Zebras feel the need to drink water very often. In regions where water is scarce, they use their sharp sense of smell and dig a hole to reach fresh water. In moments of danger, mature zebras push young zebras into the middle of the herd to protect them. As the zebras run together, young animals always remain inside the herd and run close to their mothers for better protection.

GIRAFFES: LIKE SPECKLED TOWERS

Often reaching a height of five to six metres (196 to 236 inches), you could find a resemblance between giraffes and speckled towers. The longest part of a giraffe is its neck. Its long neck enables it to reach the remotest branches on trees and feed by grazing on the sprouts and leaves. These thorny plants, which the giraffes don't chew, first go directly into their four-compartment stomach. Then they regurgitate them back to the mouth, where the giraffe chews them. Finally, they swallow them again and send them to another compartment in their stomach.

However, there is something very interesting about this process. As we have recently mentioned, giraffes regurgitate thorny plants from their stomachs back to their mouths to be chewed. But, as you may imagine, this is rather a long journey. The food needs to travel a distance of three or four metres (118 to 157 inches) in the long neck of the giraffe. As you can also imagine, it is unlikely that the food could proceed to its destination on its own. You

are curious about how giraffes could manage this, right? Let us explain it: there is a lift-like system in a giraffe's neck that makes this possible. No doubt, it is impossible for giraffes to think, "In order to digest our food, we need to send it back to our mouths; so, we must build a lift system to accomplish this".

On the other hand, such a system could not have come about by accident. You would certainly laugh at a person who tells you, "I went to that vacant area where many years ago I left some materials to construct a building. To my surprise, I found a huge building instead of the materials. No doubt, rain, snow and sun must have worked together to build this building over the years." You would also think that this man must have gone insane and would therefore feel pity for him. It would likewise be unreasonable to think that the lift system in a giraffe's neck had come into being in the same way. Such a system could not have come into existence by chance.

Furthermore, a giraffe is not a lifeless building made up of rocks, soil and mud bricks. It is a living being that runs, feels hungry and delivers babies. Is it possible that such a living being could have come into existence accidentally? Is it possible that coincidence could grant him a long neck equipped with workable systems? Of course not.

It is obvious that anything a giraffe needs has been given it at birth by Allah. Allah has specially created the mouth and stomach structures of giraffes so that

they can eat thorny, spiky plants without difficulty.

As in the case of the structure of its neck, the way a giraffe sleeps reminds us of Allah's existence. While sleeping, giraffes extend their necks towards their body. Except for a few minutes, they sleep on their feet in this position. Giraffes do not sleep all at the same time; one of them stays awake to protect the others. That a giraffe sacrifices its sleep for the sake of other giraffes and their reaching agreement about this shows us Allah's control over giraffes as in the case of all other animals.

Now, lets set aside how these speckled animals eat their food and talk about the way they drink water. Probably most people have never thought about how a giraffe bends down and drinks water without difficulty. However, our Lord, Who is the Creator of everything, wants us to ponder over such delicate systems.

First, let's make it clear that while drinking water, a serious problem awaits these long-necked creatures.

To understand this essential problem, we need to remember one thing: Do you recall what happens when you try to stand upside down? Exactly! Your face immediately turns red. That is because, our blood rushes to our heads with the effect of the force of gravity and exerts a pressure on the veins, which is called "blood pressure".

This is exactly what should happen when giraffes try to drink water. However, as you may also imagine this could be a major problem. Since giraffes are very tall animals – around five or six metres (196 to 236 inches)– the blood pressure on the head bending down from such a height becomes very great. If a human being were exposed to such high blood pressure, his brain would immediately burst.

This being the case, how do giraffes drink water without having a cerebral haemorrhage? That is because, Allah, the Creator of space, the sky, the earth and all creatures, has placed a very special mechanism inside a giraffe's head. There are little valves inside the veins of a giraffe's head. Once the height of a giraffe's head changes, these valves start to operate and prevent high blood pressure in the head.

Well, have you ever thought about why giraffes are speckled? This aesthetic appearance, in harmony with the grasslands, makes it hard for their enemies to distinguish the giraffes. Despite their giant bodies, they can thus hide from the king of the savannah, that is the lion, their foremost enemy.

In moments of danger, giraffes run at speeds of 55 to 60 kilometres (34 to 37 miles) per hour. When they begin to run, they move their heads back and forth like a pump, and curl their tails. Unlike other animals, giraffes do not take crossed steps. That is, they move their left front and hind limbs first, and then the right front and hind limbs. Owing to this, lions are hardly able to catch giraffes.

This is, no doubt, not the case for young giraffes. With their premature and weak limbs, they cannot run as fast as their mothers. For this reason, they become easy prey for lions. Yet, as we mentioned earlier, these babies always remain with their mothers. With their long limbs, mothers can give fatal kicks and thus protect them. We must stop here for a moment and think. What we call a 'giraffe' is not a human being. It is an animal. Animals do not have the faculty of thought. So, the protection giraffes and other animals provide for their young becomes possible by Allah's inspiration to them. Allah is the All-Compassionate. Regarding the mercy and compassion of Allah, a verse in the Qur'an reads as follows:

For your Lord is All-Compassionate, Most Merciful. (Surat an-Nahl: 47)

GIANT ELEPHANTS

Elephants, the largest animals on land, have two kinds of species; African and Asian elephants. African elephants are larger than the others. They may be as high as three and a half metres (137 inches) and their weight reach around six tons (12000pounds). Their fan-shaped ears are two metres (78 inches) long and one and a half metres (59 inches) wide. As you can imagine, with such a giant body, you can't keep an elephant at home as a pet.

What makes an elephant especially different is his trunk. This long trunk, similar to a garden hose, includes fifty thousand muscles. What you have read is right: "50,000" muscles! Its nostrils are at the tip of this trunk.

Elephants use their trunks to put food and water into their mouths, to lift things and, of course, to smell. This trunk is capable of holding four litres of water. They either squirt this water into their mounts and drink it or spray it on their bodies.

Surprisingly, an elephant can even pick up a tiny pea seed with its trunk –which can lift such huge things–break it in its mouth and eat it. It is really amazing that such a huge animal can accomplish such delicate operations. This "multifunctional" trunk can be used as a long finger, a trumpet or sometimes as a loudspeaker.

Besides that, elephants use their trunks to spray water on themselves to have a shower or throw dust on themselves for a dust-bath. Yet, new-born elephants fail to use their trunks. They sometimes even step on their trunks and fall down. We may find this amusing but surely these little babies do not like it. A mother elephant accompanies her young elephant for twelve years. During the first six months, she teaches the baby how to use its trunk and she never becomes bored doing this.

On both sides of their mouths, elephants have two long sharp tusks. These tusks help them to protect themselves. Also, an elephant uses one of these tusks to dig holes in the ground and find water.

The teeth of these animals–which chew fibrous plants–wear out easily. For this reason, our Lord has given them a very important characteristic: Every worn-out tooth is replaced by another in the back row.

One full-grown elephant can eat 330 kilograms (726 pounds) of plants everyday. This amount is equal to six small bales of straw. Everyday, elephants spend most of their time feeding themselves.

Now, let us give you another interesting piece of information about elephants. Have you ever thought how these huge thick-skinned animals cool themselves? As you might imagine, elephants cannot sweat because of their thick skins. Instead, they cool themselves with the help of the water and mud they see around. Of course, elephants have other methods to freshen themselves. For example, they use their ears as fans and cool their bodies with them. The thin blood veins on their ears also cool them and cause overall refreshment.

Another feature of elephants has surprised hunters and zoologists for a long time. What astonished them was the rumbling of elephants' stomachs. While rumbling, elephants' stomachs make very loud noises. Yet, what is astonishing is not the loudness of these noises but the way elephants control them. In fact these noises have nothing to do with digestion. The elephants make these noises to detect the location of their friends. More surprisingly, in the face of a danger, they all of a sudden become silent. Once they sense the threat is over, they start making noise again. Thanks to this method, elephants can communicate with one another even from four kilometres away.

The migration stories of elephants have always astonished zoologists. These animals with their

giant ears and huge bodies migrate in the dry seasons and always follow the same paths. What is even more interesting is that they clean up garbage such as chips of wood they find on their way.

Since elephants are animals that spread over vast areas of land, it is essential that they establish strong "communications" between them. Elephants do not owe this communication to their sharp sense of smell alone. Beside this, Allah has created an organ on their forehead, which makes a hoarse noise. Thanks to this organ, elephants talk to each other with a secret, coded language other animals fail to understand. These hoarse noises elephants make can reach very long distances. For this reason, this special noise that elephants make is ideal for long distance conversation.

DEER: FAMOUS FOR THEIR ANTLERS

Have you ever touched an animal with antlers? If you did, you would surely be very astonished, because the antlers emerging from the animal's hairy, soft skin are stony. You can compare an antler to your nails. The hard nails coming out of your soft skin and the way they grow so neatly probably astonish you. The way animals' antlers grow is similar to the way our nails grow, yet they are much thicker, harder and bigger.

Except for the reindeer, in general only male deer have antlers. Once the mating season is over, these antlers drop off and are renewed by others growing from beneath them.

While antlers grow, they are covered by a thin, velvet-like layer of skin. Once the antler is fully-grown, the veins are cut and thus can no longer feed the skin. At this stage, the deer abrades the skin by rubbing its antlers

against hard surfaces causing the bony structure to appear. At six years of age, their antlers become fully-developed. After this age, they begin gradually to deteriorate. The length, shape and number of branches differ from one deer to another.

You have probably asked yourself, "Why do deer have antlers?" Antlers are an important weapon for deer. With antlers they can protect themselves from enemies. Sometimes, a predator only has to see the antlers to leave the deer alone.

A male red deer draws a border around its territory by smearing a substance secreted from his scent gland. In this territory, he sets up a herd consisting of female deer (doe). He protects his herd with his antlers from his enemies. Upon the entry of an alien into his territory, he pushes him out of it either by his roars or by attempting to gore him with the antlers.

Allah has created these animals with antlers on their heads, thereby making it possible for them to protect themselves and their herds. If Allah had not given them antlers, these animals would have remained defenceless and helpless against their enemies. A male deer could not protect female deer and thus his herd couldn't be constituted. They would not have a weapon against wild animals.

Possibly, few people would ever think, "I wish some animals had a hard, bony substance having a branch-like structure on their heads, so that they could protect themselves". Even if it were the case, these people would fail to make this wish come true. Only Allah, Who has created all creatures

most beautifully, has provided deer and other animals with defence mechanisms that exactly match their needs.

In the Qur'an, Allah reminds us this fact:

Say: 'In whose hand is the dominion over everything, He who gives protection and from whom no protection can be given, if you have any knowledge?' (Surat al-Muminun: 88)

As stated in the following verses, the protector of all creatures is Allah alone.

... Your Lord is the Preserver of all things. (Surah Saba': 21)

KANGAROOS AND THEIR POCKETS

You may ask, "Is it possible that an animal could have a pocket?" Surprisingly, kangaroos have a "pouch" on their bellies where baby kangaroos are fed and protected during their development.

The appearance of a joey (baby kangaroo) whose head appears from its mother's pouch arouses feelings of compassion in us. This baby, coming out of the womb when it was only one centimetre (0.393 inches) long—that is before it was fully-developed—reached its mother's pouch after a three minute journey.

There are four different nipples in the pouch of the mother. The new-born sucks the nipple that issues a milk with just the right temperature and amount of fat for a new-born. The other three nipples, on the other hand, contain milk meeting the needs of an older baby. In a few weeks, the new-born stops suckling its nipple and finds another nipple from which issues a milk prepared for its own needs. As it grows older, it finds a third nipple with the type of milk specially prepared for its needs.

Children! At this point, you must ask yourself the questions, "How can a baby kangaroo one centimetre long know the right nipple that would meets its needs?", "How has the mother kangaroo placed milk in her four nipples with such different ingredients?" What is more, the milk the new-born baby sucks is hotter than the other milk from the other nipples. Their ingredients are also different. This being the case, how did the mother kangaroo manage to heat this milk? How has she added the necessary ingredients to this milk?

Remember, it is not the mother who has accomplished all these things. The mother kangaroo does not even know that the milk issuing from the nipples is different. It is unlikely that she could compute the temperature of the milk produced by her nipples. She cannot manage to provide each nipple with different kinds of milk. She cannot even know that they are different. She is only a kangaroo living under Allah's watchful care. Her baby's needs are taken care of by Allah. Our Lord, the All-Compassionate and Most Merciful, has placed the most appropriate milk in the most appropriate place for the babies, that is, in the mother's pouch.

A baby kangaroo spends its first six and a half months in this pouch. After spending the next eight months both in the pouch and outside, it leaves it once and for all. Meanwhile, before the first joey leaves the pouch, a new brother or sister crawls into the pouch. They both live in the same pouch for a long time, without giving any harm to one another. Each joey sucks on the nipple with the milk containing just the right ingredients for their needs. Then, how do the two siblings know which nipple to suck? The answer is obvious: by Allah's inspiration.

Kangaroos are awesome with their huge bodies; the body is one and a half metres long and the tail one metre (39 inches) long. Thanks to their long hind limbs, the kangaroo family can traverse a distance of eight metres in only a moment. While running, they maintain balance by their big strong tails. Do you think their feet have become large by coincidence? Or, do you think their mother estimated that they would need large hind limbs to leap? Of course, none of these give us the right answer. Nothing has come into existence accidentally. Allah, the One Who creates everything according to the needs of creatures, has also created kangaroos like all other creatures in their most perfect form.

THE KOALA:
THE SLEEPYHEAD

We always remember the greyish furred koalas wrapping their arms and legs around the trunks of eucalyptus trees. This sight of koalas is indeed very lovely. Meanwhile, you may wonder why we call a koala "the sleepyhead". Let's remind ourselves right away that koalas sleep 18 hours a day!

The fore and hind paws of koalas enable them to spend a great part of their lives on eucalyptus trees. This is the way Allah created their paws!

Koalas can quickly climb trees with their long curled arms, and sharp claws and paws that hold tightly on to the trees. The two fingers of their fore-paws are separated from the other three. If we compare a human hand to theirs, then we must talk about two thumbs. These thumbs, which greatly differ from other fingers, help them to cling to small branches. Like a hook, koalas thrust their claws into trees and thus hold on to the soft and smooth surfaces of tree trunks. With their four paws, they can readily clutch tree branches, just like we clutch a stick, and climb trees after they wrap their paws around

their branches. These are what makes a koala's life on trees easy!

Although koalas are known to be lazy, they can move very quickly on trees. They can even jump from one branch to another, covering a distance of a metre (39 inches) in a leap. Female koalas give birth to a single baby in two years and, like kangaroos, they carry it in their pouch. During the first months, the baby koala remains in its mother's pouch. After this period, the baby hitches a piggyback ride for a year. The mother picks a favourite tree in the eucalyptus forest for its home because she eats eucalyptus leaves – and that's about all she eats! That is why you can only find koalas in Australia, where eucalyptus trees are legion.

Although there are more than 600 species of eucalyptus tree in Australia, koalas only eat certain leaves from 35 of them. Koalas can't live just anywhere because, apart from being a store of leaves, the eucalyptus trees constitute a unique shelter for them.

There are many kinds of koala species. Each species feed on a different kind of eucalyptus leaf. If you are planning to move a koala away, you need also to take the eucalyptus leaves on which he feeds with you. Apart from their diets, koalas rarely climb down eucalyptus trees because they are hardly able to move around on the ground. The eucalyptus tree's leaves constitute different chemical substances. These substances are poisonous and dangerous for all animals except for koalas. Before swallowing, koalas grind these leaves with their teeth. The harmful elements in the leaves are filtered in the koala's liver and expelled from the body. By the will of Allah, this food, which is extremely poisonous for other animals, does not harm koalas. Therefore, koalas can eat about a kilogram (2.204 pounds) of poisonous leaves everyday without trouble. Koalas even get their water from these leaves. At certain times of the year, two thirds of the eucalyptus leaf consists of water. Therefore, only feeding on eucalyptus leaves, a koala can survive for months without drinking water. The tops of eucalyptus trees are vulnerable to wind. For this reason, koalas have very thick fur.

This harmony between a poisonous plant and an animal shows us that koalas and eucalyptus tree have been created by the same Creator. This Creator, Who creates everything perfectly, is surely Allah, the Lord of all the worlds.

PLAYFUL CATS WHO WANT TO BE CHERISHED

Cats are self-reliant animals that live without attachments. They never submit to their owners' wishes as do pet dogs. As you have most probably seen, cats meow when they feel hungry, rub against your feet when they

want to be caressed, purr with pleasure when they are patted and convey many similar messages by the way they act.

Do you know that cats have perfect eyesight at night?

Yes, even in a dimly lit place these furry creatures can see. Allah has created their eyes differently from other eyes. In the dark, their eyes' pupils become larger and rounder to receive as much light as possible. This gives them keen eyesight.

This aside, a cat's eye has an additional layer behind the retina. Passing through the retina, light reaches this layer and is then reflected back to the retina. Light passes through the retina twice since this layer reflects the light back. Therefore, unlike human beings, cats can see very well in dimly lit or dark places.

Have you ever thought why cats' eyes sparkle at night?

This is related to the additional layer in cats' eyes we have just mentioned. As you know, this layer reflects the light like a mirror. It is this reflected light that makes their eyes look sparkling.

Do you know the features of a cat's paws?

In moments of danger, these tiny paws turn into predatory claws.

What makes them dangerous are the sharp nails they hide in their paws.

Why do they always fall on their feet?

You know that cats always fall on their four feet, even when they fall from a height. The actual reason cats fall on their feet is that they use their tails to maintain their balance while falling and thus adjust the centres of gravity of their bodies and land on their paws.

The One Who has given them such a feature that will ensure the safety of these animals that enjoy climbing trees and wandering on high places is our Mighty Lord, the All-Compassionate, the Most Merciful.

THE KING OF THE JUNGLE: THE LION

The lion belongs to the cat family and is very predatory. With his long trunk, short legs, large head, strong appearance and majesty, he deserves the title "the King of the Jungle" even though lions do not really live in the jungle but in the savannah.

A lion's tail is about three metres (118 inches) long. He is approximately one metre (39 inches) long and he weighs around 230 kilograms (506 pounds). To put it another way, lions are really big cats that are one and a half to two metres (59 to 78 inches) longer than you.

Male lions have manes. This soft hair surrounds the face and covers the back of the head, neck and shoulders and extends from the chest to the belly. This mane gives the male lion a very imposing appearance indeed. The mane that Allah has given male lions makes them look much stronger

and more impressive than they actually are.

Lions spend all day lying or sleeping under the shadow of rocks or trees and wake up at night to hunt. Lions possess perfect eyesight at night and can easily see their prey. There is a special design in a lion's eyes which means that they collect as much light as possible. Pupils and lenses that are relatively larger than other animals' eyes make lions good hunters in the animal kingdom. Allah has given them features which are most appropriate in relation to their environment.

You can hear a lion roaring in particular at night, the time of their hunting, and before dawn. When the lion roars, life on the savannah almost stops; the wolf stops howling and the leopard stops growling. Everybody remains silent and listens to the king while the monkeys climb the top branches of trees, screaming as loud as they can.

WILD CATS: TIGERS

Never think for a moment that they are compliant like a cat! They are very wild and strong. They are the strongest of the cat family.

New-born tigers open their eyes only two days after they are born. Although she is very wild towards other animals, the mother tiger is very sensitive and caring towards her cubs. She suckles them for a period of six weeks. Then, she gradually teaches them how to hunt and find their food.

After this period of education, the young cub grows into a strong adult that can move very fast. At one leap, he can cover a distance of four metres (157 inches). Now, open your arms wide. The distance from the fingertip of one of your hands to the fingertip of the other is about a metre. Four times this is the distance that a tiger covers in only one jump.

Tigers can camouflage themselve–adaptation to environment–a feature of which they are unaware. Their fur, very much in harmony with the natural colours of the environment in which they live, is extraordinarily suitable for camouflage in the jungle. This way, they can secretly approach their prey. Besides, these colours give tigers very aesthetically beautiful and impressive features. The lines on their fur and cheeks as well as the shapes of their eyebrows differ from one tiger to another.

Tigers respect each other's hunting territories. A tiger marks its territory by leaving a scent it secretes on the bushes. This odour warns other tigers of the existence of another tiger's territory.

The unusual features of tigers are not limited to these. Unlike other cat species, these wild-cats like water very much. Furthermore, in spite of their huge bodies, they are great swimmers. Like all other creatures, Allah has granted tigers awe-inspiring characteristics.

Little baby tigers are very cute and thus arouse compassion in us. Despite being very wild animals, Allah has inspired mother tigers to be very compassionate and merciful towards their babies.

MASKED PANDAS

You have most probably seen this animal that looks like a huge toy. Do you know that these animals eat bamboo and nothing else? An adult panda, for example, eats about 15 kilograms (33 pounds) of bamboo a day. This makes six tons (12000 pounds) of bamboo a year. For this reason, they eat all day long. They are insatiable, aren't they?

Pandas have a very interesting feature. Now, have a look at your hand. You have five fingers, right? But pandas have six fingers. Our Lord, Who makes everything easy for every living being, has given pandas six fingers and enabled them to grasp their food tightly, so that they can eat easily.

Pandas always live in cold wet places. Because of this, they deliver their babies in cave-like places. Baby pandas are blind and toothless and to us look like little toys. Usually born in September, they are 10 centimetres (4 inches) high and weigh only 142 grams. New-born pandas grow up very fast and are 800 times smaller than their mothers. But after nine months, they weigh 27 kilograms (59 pounds). Remember that a six year old human being only weighs 27 kilograms (59 pounds)!

Pandas are not ferocious animals. They only scratch trees with their paws in order to clean and rasp their nails. To avoid their enemies, they climb trees with their huge bodies. Pandas are very calm animals. While they are asleep, an approaching human being does not bother them. That is, if you encounter a sleeping panda one day, there is no reason not to caress it!

BEARS ARE FOND OF HONEY

Bears, famous for their shaggy coats and eating honey, have a very poor sense of sight and hearing. So, how do they find honey, you will ask? Well, by means of the long noses Allah has given them. Their noses, that is, their keen sense of smell ensures that they find the best honey around.

You probably know that bears have a very awkward appearance. But don't think for a moment that they are slow. Indeed, they can run at 48 kilometres (30 miles) per hour. We also need to mention that they are very strong. With their two to three metres (78 to 118 inches) long bodies, some bear species climb the top branches of trees and spend time there. Bears, who usually feed on plants, even climb up to 30 metres (1181 inches) high to find food.

Once a bear finds a beehive, it strikes it a few times with its paws, which causes all the bees in the hive to escape. Then they eat the honey with appetite. But you should never try this! Because, bees will sting you all over and make you sick. But, the coat our Lord has given to bears protects them against the bees. So, they can easily reach honey without any trouble.

Bears that hibernate in autumn never leave their secure dens where they lie covered with dry branches and grasses until spring. Before hibernation, they eat a lot, especially cones and chestnuts, so that the fat layer underlying their skin thickens. They have to store fat in their body. That is because before spring they will lose so much weight. If a man lost so much weight, he would die outright. But bears can survive even though they lose so much of their weight.

Delivery is another reason that bears spend time in their caves. Bears usually give birth to three cubs, and they feed them with milk until spring. During that time they never leave their caves. Bear cubs are born blind, toothless and hairless. Once the cubs are out of the cave, the mother bear must protect them. Otherwise, they might be killed by hunters or male bears.

Our Lord, Who is the All-Compassionate and Merciful, meets the needs of all creatures and protects them. Likewise, He has provided cute bear cubs with everything they need to survive and not be hurt. He has secured their protection by means of their strong mothers who never leave them.

GIANT SNOWMEN: POLAR BEARS

If you saw a polar bear, which is one of the biggest animals on earth, you might assume it to be a giant snowman. This giant snowman weighs around 800 kilograms (1763 pounds) and is about two and a half metres (98 inches) long. Put the weight of ten men together and they will weigh a polar bear!

The polar bear has some amazing features which allow it to live at the north pole. Despite the polar climate, glaciers and snowstorms, as a miracle from Allah, a thick layer of fat underlying its skin protects the polar bear from cold. Its fur is thick, dense, long and fluffy. Have you ever thought about why polar bears with such characteristics do not live in the deserts of Africa? Certainly, the answer is that Allah has created him with features suited to the environment in which he lives. Think for a moment! If he were in the desert, he could hardly withstand the hot climate of the desert for a minute.

What makes the polar bear different from all other bears is that it is not very fond of hibernation. Only the female polar bears, especially those pregnant, hibernate for a long period. Allah, "ar-Razzaq, the One Who continuously provides sustenance to all living beings," has made food available for the new-born cub. The milk of polar bears contains a high amount of fat. This fatty milk is what the cubs need most. They grow very fast, thanks to this fatty milk, and get ready to go out of their caves in the spring.

Have you heard that the polar bear is a very good swimmer and diver? That is true! The polar bear is a skilled swimmer and diver. While

swimming, it uses its forelegs. That it can use its legs as paddles is something by which Allah has made life easy for him. Apart from this, in water, it can close its nostrils and keep its eyes open, and its webbed feet, similar to those of ducks, make it a good swimmer.

The polar bear lives in the coldest regions of the world such as the North Pole, Northern Canada and Northern Siberia. But the feet of the polar bear never become cold. You could hardly keep your feet or hands on ice for more than a couple of minutes. Surprisingly, however, the polar bear does not even feel this cold since its feet are covered with thick fur. Allah gave it just the right features so that it would not be affected by the cold. If it were covered with skin similar to that of human beings, it would never survive. Moreover, the fatty layer ten centimetres (four inches) thick under its skin provides heat insulation. Therefore, in icy waters, it can swim 2000 kilometres (1242 miles) at a speed of 10 to 11 kilometres (6 to 7 miles) per hour.

Do you know why the colour of polar bears is white or off-white? It is hard to notice the white polar bear among the white snow-covered glaciers and the frozen wastes of the north that extend for thousands of kilometres. Imagine how difficult it would be for it to hide itself if its colour were as black as a crow or as colourful as one of the parrots living in the tropical forests.

Polar bears' sense of smell is so keen that they can readily smell a seal that hides under a layer of snow one and a half metre (59 inches) thick.

While hunting, polar bears also employ some tactics. Now, visualise a polar bear with its snow-white fur looking like a snowman. Do you think anyone would notice it if it lays on the snow?
If you only considered its white fur, you might have said "yes". But, remember that the polar bear also has a black nose. On white snow, this nose makes perfect camouflage impossible. But the polar bear does something very intelligent and eliminates this problem. It covers its nose with its white forepaws. Totally hidden in the snow, it awaits its prey's approach.

This point deserves particular attention because for a polar bear to employ hunting tactics it must be intelligent. Think for a moment: the polar bear is aware that its white colour is a perfect match for the environment in which it lives. Moreover, it is wise enough to realise that it needs to cover

its black nose, the only obstacle to its camouflage. As you can also imagine, it is unlikely that the polar bear would have found this tactic after a few unsuccessful hunting experiences! Bears are inspired by Allah and are taught to act in this way. Because, like all other creatures, they are also under the protection of Allah.

FAST SWIMMERS: SEALS

These cute animals, which most of you know from television and from circuses, spend most of their lives in the water. They are very good swimmers and divers. They are just as happy and comfortable in water and on glaciers as we are on land. Even in spring, the temperature of their habitat remains around −5 degrees Centigrade (23F). While we have to put on clothes and take many precautions, they don't feel cold at all. Because their fur and the fat they store in their body prevent them from being cold.

Seals live in crowded groups. How do you think a mother seal recognises her young in the group? That is easy. After delivery, the mother seal gives her cub a welcome kiss from which she becomes acquainted with the baby's smell and distinguishes it from all other cub seals.

At birth, a kind of oil called the "baby oil" covers the cub's body. Thanks to this oil, the little body always stays warm. This oil is so dense that during the swimming lessons the cub takes from its mother it floats on the surface of water as if wearing a life buoy. That is because this oil is lighter than water. Swimming lessons for the cub take about two weeks. Once it is over, the seal cub becomes entirely self-reliant.

As is in the case of all other animals, seals are also given by Allah features suiting their environment. This is another sign showing us the mercy of our Lord.

PENGUINS IN THEIR TUXEDOS

Waddling penguins are actually a bird species that can't fly. They form big colonies. They have been created so perfectly by Allah that they can even survive in a region where the temperature can sometimes be as low as –88 degrees Centigrade (-126F). Think for a moment: we put on our jumpers, socks, gloves, coats etc., in winter. But, penguins need none of these. They do not even wear shoes. However, they can easily walk on ice without slipping. This apart, penguins do not have houses, they simply live on ice. Don't they ever feel cold? The answer is "No", because Allah has especially created them in a way that they can survive in an icy environment.

The body features of penguins are very different from those of human beings. Shall we have a look at them?

In winter, these cute creatures, that belong to a group of 400000 members, decide to migrate south from the coast further into the icy cold of Antarctica! This consensus they reach is a great miracle in itself. That penguins understand the approach of winter, that they collectively decide on a destination and time to migrate and their compliance with all these decisions without objections from any of the members can only be explained by Allah's overall control of them. Otherwise, it would be impossible for thousands of penguins to reach agreement and migrate to another habitat.

The migratory season is also the mating season for penguins. At this time of the year what a penguin primarily does is choose a mate for itself. The second step is to learn the song of the mate in order not to lose her. In other words, the male penguin has the ability to distinguish a specific sound from all other sounds. Remember that it is only by the Will of Allah that a penguin–a creature bereft of wisdom and intelligence as understood by humans–can choose a mate for himself among four hundred thousand penguins and recognise her voice.

This sensitivity in distinguishing voices also holds true for baby penguins. They can recognise their parents by their voices alone. If there were no such distinction among these animals, who are very much alike one another, chaos would be inevitable. The unique order established by Allah for penguins and

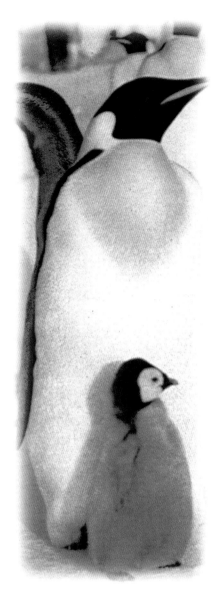

the features given to them secure an orderly life for penguins.

After mating, the female penguin lays only one egg. The responsibility of the male penguin is to incubate this egg. At a temperature as low as −30 degrees Centigrade (-22 F), he tries to fulfil this responsibility without moving for 65 days. This is indeed a tough time for the male penguin. Because he guards the egg, he has no chance to hunt. The mother penguin, on the other hand, leaves to find food for the coming baby.

Can you imagine waiting for 65 days without eating anything? For a human being, the result would certainly be death. However, penguins make this sacrifice without displaying any impatience or boredom, and fulfil the service inspired in them by Allah until they complete it.

After an incubation period of two months, the male penguin loses 1/3 of his weight. In the same case, a human being of 60 kilograms (132 pounds) would lose 20 kilograms (44 pounds). After the egg hatches, the baby penguin spends its first two months between his parent's feet. This protection is vital for the baby because leaving this warm place for only a couple of minutes would result in death. It is surely Allah Who inspires the parents to protect their baby in this way. In this, we once again witness that Allah is the Protector of all living beings. Furthermore, the penguin colony, which has 400000 members, displays a perfect example of solidarity by gathering together and sticking close to one another to protect themselves and each other from the polar climate. By such precautions, these animals manage to keep their colony warm because they decrease the heat loss by half. Meanwhile, they take those penguins remaining on the outer edge of the circle one by one into the colony, and ensure that they also are warm. Penguins have lived in great harmony for generations and they will continue to maintain this order without even one member raising an objection to it.

FISHER PUFFINS

You might never have heard this animal's name before, but, as you get to know him, you will both enjoy him and come to like him a lot.

Most people assume the puffin to be a kind of penguin. However, the puffin is actually a different kind of bird. Unlike a penguin, a puffin can fly, which is the greatest difference between them. Puffins live at the North Pole whereas penguins live at the South Pole. What they have in common is that both species can easily adapt themselves to a cold environment.

Puffins have very interesting lives. The mother and father puffins never leave one another all through their lives, and raise a young puffin every year.

In the breeding season, the lines on their beaks, which are usually dull, turn a bright colour. Yet, this colour change does not occur accidentally. These lines, which serve a particular purpose, have been given especially to puffins by Allah. Thanks to these lines, puffins use their beaks like flags and thus communicate with one another over long distances.

Can you make a single line appear on your nose when you want to do so? Let's assume that there exists such a line at birth. Can you turn it into an indistinct pattern or make it disappear? We can already hear you saying "No", because you already know that it is only our Lord Who can accomplish such artistry!

It is easy for our Lord to create various kinds of birds and to endow them with features suiting their habitats. Similarly, it is easy for Him to create a line on their beaks or to make it disappear.

Allah, Who has created puffins so beautifully, has also given them some other striking features. Now, let's continue examining these features:

Once they are six weeks old, young puffins leave their parents and begin to fly over the open sea.

A healthy puffin lives for about 25 years.

Puffins can dive very deep. Do you know what awaits a human being who wants to dive as deep as a puffin? First of all, he needs an oxygen supply. Besides that, he risks his life since the pressure on one increases as one dives deeper and deeper. For this reason, diving requires great mastery. How did puffins learn the techniques necessary to keep their breath in deep water and to get back to the surface again? Our Lord once again shows us His sublimity and the uniqueness of His artistry in creation.

Here is another beautiful aspect of the puffin: The mouth structure of puffins enables them to hold many little fish in their mouths. Indeed, a puffin can hold 62 fish at a time. The mother has only one purpose in holding so many fish in her mouth: to feed her babies! So, if you see a puffin with many fish in its mouth, remember that it has a baby to feed.

SOVEREIGNS OF THE SKIES:
BIRDS

Do they not see the birds suspended in mid-air up in the sky?
Nothing holds them there except Allah. There are certainly
Signs in that for people who have faith. (Surat an-Nahl: 79)

Like everyone else, you have most probably wanted to fly like a bird. Looking at birds, you may think flying is easy, but it is not as easy as it seems!

A bird uses great energy when it takes wing because it has to lift all its body with its tiny wings. Yet, once it is up in the air, Allah has made it easy for it to remain aloft without expending too much effort. Birds can fly for a long time by allowing themselves to rely on the wind. This way, they hardly tire since they consume very little energy. When the effect produced by the wind diminishes, they begin to flap their wings again. By means of this feature Allah has given birds, they can cover very long distances and migrate to remote destinations.

There are bird species that can cover distances between 1000 to 40000 kilometres (621 and 24840 miles). Considering that it is 40000 kilometres (24840 miles) around the earth, you can conceive better the long distances covered by birds. Passing over the oceans, they have no chance to take a break and rest. How birds maintain their direction during their thousands of kilometres long flights still remains a mystery. Each year, birds migrate to their destinations without losing their ways. This holds true for young birds as well as adults.

It is interesting that birds' legs, so slender and little in comparison to their bodies, can carry their entire bodies. It is amazing that so many muscles, veins and nerves can exist in such a slender leg! If birds' legs were thicker and relatively more bulky, it would be more difficult for them to fly.

Almost all birds sleep on one leg. This does not upset their balance since their body weight is concentrated on this one leg. Allah has created birds with the features that enable them to maintain such a delicate balance.

One of the best sensory organs of birds is their eyes. Apart from the ability to fly, Allah has also granted birds superior sight, because, flight, which is itself a miracle, becomes extremely dangerous unless it is supported by superior sight. Birds can see objects at a distance much better than human beings and have a wider angle of vision. Noticing the dangers beforehand, they accurately determine their speed and the direction of their flight.

Birds' eyes remain fixed in the eye sockets, that is, they can't move their eyes as human beings can. However, they can widen the angle of vision by rapidly turning their heads and necks.

Furthermore, night birds such as owls

have very large eyes. Some special cells in their eyes are sensitive to dim light. The vision of barred owls, for example, is 100 times keener than that of human beings. Thanks to this feature, owls can see and hunt very well at night.

The eyes of water fowl, on the other hand, have been created for clear underwater vision. While we can't keep our eyes open underwater for even 45 seconds, water birds can easily catch insects and molluscs in water as they plunge their heads into it. Since this is the only way for them to feed themselves, they must have clear vision underwater. For this reason, Allah has created a special structure in their eyes, which permits seeing underwater. Thanks to this structure, these birds don't have dim sight underwater; they see very clearly and can immediately swim towards their prey.

Hearing is also very important for birds. Some birds have eardrums that enable them to hear very low sounds. Being able to see very well in darkness and underwater and being able to hear very low sounds are abilities that human beings don't possess. Indeed, we don't need these faculties very

much, because, we can readily lead our lives without them. However, it is impossible for birds to eat, feed their young, and continue their lives and their race without these abilities.

The ears of owls are very sensitive to sound. They have better hearing than human beings. There are hair-like bristles on both sides of an owls' face, which collect sound waves and send them into the inner ear. These bristles also separate one ear from the other and thus the sound coming from the right is largely heard by the right ear. Moreover, the ears are not positioned symmetrically on the head. One ear is higher than the other. So, the owl perceives the sounds from different directions and, although he does not see it, he correctly determines the location of the creature that makes the sound. This is a very important advantage in snowy weather, when it becomes hard to find prey.

Some birds produce various voices to mislead their predators. For instance, many bird species that make nests in holes in trees hiss like snakes when they are disturbed. So, predators attempting to attack the nest stay away from it, assuming that there is a snake in it.

Besides, our Lord has given some bird species webbed feet to help them swim faster when they are in water. These webbed feet are similar to flippers. If you have ever worn flippers while swimming, you will know how it helps you swim. Some species have such flippers at birth.

Some bird species build fake nests to protect their young from predators. Especially in Africa and India, animals which feed on bird eggs are legion. For this reason, African wrens protect their eggs in a real nest surrounded by many fake nests. The snakes living on trees in tropical regions are very poisonous. For this reason, the entrances to the nests of the penduline-tit colonies peculiar to that region are secret and complicated. Moreover, as another precaution, these birds make their nests on acacia trees with densely thorny branches, and deceive their predators with many empty – fake – nests.

Have you ever paid attention to the beaks of the birds that fly around us everyday? Allah created these beaks, which vary from one species to another, with very important functions. Birds' beaks have the most appropriate shapes that enable them to feed in their environments. The beaks of birds that feed on fish, for example, are generally long and ladle-shaped, making them good fishers. If the bird feeds on plants, then the beak of the bird has a perfect match with the plant on which it feeds. As these examples show, Allah's creation is flawless and complete because He gives all creatures the features they need.

LONG-LEGGED STORKS

In the warm days of the spring, some of the large white birds we see in the sky while flying our kites are storks. The stork is a big, migratory bird that is one to one and a half metres (60 inches) in height, with large white wings and a long black tail. Its beak and long legs are red, giving them a lovely appearance.

One of the most striking characteristics of storks is the way they fly. While flying, they extend their heads forward and push their legs backward. This aesthetic style of storks enables them to fly much faster by cleaving the air aerodynamically. Every year, storks migrate to warm regions because they are vulnerable to cold. That is why when we see storks arriving, we also receive the glad tidings of hot summer days. In the summer season, storks live in the temperate regions that extend from Europe to North Africa and from Turkey to Japan. Before the weather cools, they migrate to the southern hemisphere, tropical Africa and India.

It is amazing that storks know it becomes warm in the southern

hemisphere at that time of the year. This is a miracle. Yet, what is more amazing is that, after six monts, exactly at spring, storks fly all the way back, covering distances of thousands of kilometres, to find the nests they left behind.

This is astonishing indeed.

Storks find the nests they made the previous year and settle there again. But how do they find their old nest right away after such a long time? Do they use a compass in order not to lose their way? Of course, such a good memory and excellent sense of direction have been inspired in storks by their Lord, Allah.

In addition, these stick-legged animals do not travel overseas because they need some land on which to stop and rest when they become exhausted. For this reason, they prefer travelling across seas close to land such as the Bosphorus, the Straits of Gibraltar and the Suez Canal.

Storks do not avoid human beings and they build their nests on the tops of buildings, trees and chimneys. Usually flocks of storks migrate together. When they arrive in Europe, they spend some time there. Ordinarily, during the first week of April, the male stork builds a nest from branches. As we mentioned earlier, he chooses the same place every year. He carefully protects the nest and occasionally leaves it to search for food. Some kinds of stork make their nests in swamps on top of branches and they live in groups. You can find twelve large stork nests on the very same cypress tree. The fact that birds live in communities has been also pointed out in the Qur'an:

There is no creature crawling on the earth or flying creature, flying on its wings, who are not communities just like yourselves – We have not omitted anything from the Book – then they will be gathered to their Lord. (Surat al-An'am: 38)

Do you know how storks communicate with each other? They communicate with each other not by making different vocal sounds but by making noises with their beaks. They explain many things to each other with "tap tap" sounds.

Here is another question: do you know that storks dance? When they get together, the male stork and his spouse dance by tapping their beaks and flapping their wings. During this dance, the male stork tries to attract the female stork's attention. If you consider that a stork is almost the same height as a man, you can imagine how impressive this dance is.

Not all storks are the same height. The smallest kind of stork is the Asian and African openbill. When they close their bills, only the two ends of the bill close together. The remaining parts remain apart. This kind of beak enables the stork to eat snails and mussels more easily.

That Allah creates every living being with various capabilities in a beautiful fashion is something that helps us to have a deeper faith in Him and helps us to see His might and perfect creation in everything we see around us and to understand His signs.

A PINK BIRD: THE FLAMINGO

You have probably seen a long-necked, long-legged pink bird on TV. This bird is called the "flamingo". Flamingos leave their eggs in shallow muddy lakes. What is interesting is that the female flamingo leaves her egg in the nest she makes out of quick-drying mud.

Imagine yourself in the flamingo's shoes and assume that you want to make a nest for yourself. You need primarily to discover which type of mud dries more quickly and find where the young flamingo can hatch more easily. Meanwhile, you need to find the answers to many questions such as "is it better to put the egg under the sun or in the shade?" However, each flamingo knows how to accomplish this. Moreover, despite her long legs offering no comfort to her, she incubates for a month and waits for her young to hatch.

If you were in her shoes, would you dare to sit on the egg with your giant body? Could you estimate whether the egg would be broken, if you sat on it? Surely, it would be very difficult for you to know all these things. However, all flamingos estimate these things without planning or trial and error because, they are taught so by their Lord.

Flamingos attract our attention with their eye-catching colours and long necks, and they are also very good swimmers. Their webbed feet help them to swim. By means of these webbed feet, which have a wide flat structure, they can walk easily without sinking even on soft mud. Furthermore, the webs between their toes provide a wide surface, so that flamingos can propel themselves through the water. As we have seen, flamingos have been created with all the details necessary for their survival.

ELEGANT SWANS

White swans swim proudly with their elegant, slender necks and big bodies. Everybody admires the nobility of their appearance. Since they are so beautiful, they are like ornaments on the creation.

*You might have heard the tale of the ugly duckling. As is told in this tale, young swans are very ugly when they hatch. They have a brown or cream colour. Newly hatched young swans–called signets–have short necks and are covered with dense feathers. Within a couple of hours of the eggs cracking open, they can run and swim. Their parents look after them meticulously for a couple of months. Finally, the ugly duckling turns into a magnificent swan. These baby swans' ability to swim in such a short time and their transformation into beautiful creatures is possible only because of the perfection of Allah's artistry in creation. As we are informed by Allah in a verse; "**He who has created all things in the best possible way!**". (Surat as-Sajdah: 7)*

"The trumpeter" is a kind of swan that sits on her developing eggs to keep them warm. Occasionally she stands up and turns her eggs. This way, she ensures that the heat disperses everywhere equally. Certainly, it is Allah Who inspires swans with the kind of care their eggs need.

Owing to the ability Allah has bestowed on them, swans move very fast both in water and in the air. Swans feel more comfortable in water and can swim very fast, thanks to their webbed feet.

Swans start to migrate when the weather becomes cold, and they fly at high altitudes, lining up in a row. On their route, to puncture the strong wind currents they encounter, they fly in a "V" formation. By means of this wise formula, they fly much faster and move along without becoming so tired. Of course, it is impossible for swans to discover such a method, which would require an advanced knowledge of aerodynamics (aerodynamics is the study of forces and resulting motion of objects through the air) and physics. They fly so because Allah, Who possesses the knowledge of everything, has inspired them so.

Have they not looked at the birds above them, with wings outspread and folded back? Nothing holds them up but the All-Merciful. He sees all things. (Surat al-Mulk: 19)

Swans feed on the plants they find at the bottoms of swamps, creeks and ponds. Their long necks help them to reach food. Like ducks, they can plunge into the water and encounter no difficulty in short dives. There is a useful side to swans' plucking plants: Some plants grow and mature as soil is puffed up. As swans scrap at the bottom of the water to find food, they make plants grow abundantly. Thus, by the Will of Our Lord, they cause the growth of ample amounts of plants. This way, by making use of swans, our Lord ensures the growth of plants.

OSTRICHES
(SO BIG THAT THEY CAN'T FLY!)

Ostriches are the biggest birds in the world. They are taller than us. An ostrich is approximately two and a half metres (98 inches) tall and weighs 120 kilograms (264 pounds).

These birds, which live in colonies in Central Africa, can't fly. Instead, Allah has given them a different ability so that they can escape from their predators: They run very fast with their long legs. They run so fast that no man can keep up with them. Ostriches are the fastest two-legged animals in the animal kingdom and they reach speeds of 70 kilometres (43 miles) per hour. And now let us tell you something very interesting. Do you know that ostriches have only two toes on their feet? What is more, one of these toes is considerably bigger than the other. And ostriches run only on their big toes.

Besides that, thanks to their long legs enabling them to run fast, ostriches are very good warriors. To protect themselves against their enemies, they kick their predators.

The egg of the biggest bird in the world is also the biggest bird egg in the world. They dig a very deep hole in the sand and place all their eggs in

it. But when they lay more than 10 to 12 eggs, they need to adjust the size of the hole accordingly. If the ostrich dug this hole in soil instead of sand, this would take a longer time, causing the birds to consume more energy. Indeed, digging sand is much easier than soil. You may even dig sand with your hands whereas you need a shovel to dig soil. For this reason, ostriches, by the inspiration of Allah, prefer digging in the sand rather than in soil and thus consume minimal energy. Then they cover their eggs with sand again without difficulty.

Another interesting piece of information about ostriches is that the care of all eggs in a flock is undertaken by a single female ostrich. But, since the nest can shelter only a limited number of eggs, the female ostrich gives priority to her own eggs. Ostriches distinguish their own eggs by the air pores on the egg shells.

The baby ostriches emerging from the eggs are utterly defenceless. At any moment, they could be attacked by a predatory bird. Yet, when new-born ostriches feel endangered, they lie on the ground and act as if dead. This way, their predators, assuming they are dead, do not attack them. Without exception, all baby ostriches employ this defence mechanism.

It is impossible for a new-born chick to think up such a tactic or to learn how to employ it! So, how could a baby bird that has only recently opened its eyes to the world act as if dead? The answer is obvious. Our Lord, the One Who teaches and educates every living being, has also taught these little babies such an effective defence mechanism, so that they can protect themselves.

THE RESPLENDENT PEACOCK
(THE MOST ELEGANT BIRD
IN THE ANIMAL KINGDOM)

If you have ever been to a zoo, you must certainly have seen a peacock with its magnificent plumage. The most important characteristic of peacocks is that they have a tail adorned with colours of unimaginable

beauty. Yet, only male peacocks have such a magnificent tail.

With its blue head and neck, the peacock also has gilded green feathers on its tail. These beautiful feathers, called "quill feathers", have round tips with small spots.

However, you cannot always witness this magnificent sight. You have to wait for the peacock's breeding season. The male peacock only opens his tail like a fan and displays its beauty in order to attract the female peacock's attention.

Here, we need to ponder over the following: How can a male peacock, who is unable to see himself, be so sure that he will look beautiful and attractive when he displays his tail? Someone must have taught him this; is that right? No doubt, our Lord, Who has created such beauty, has also inspired the peacock on how to use it.

Could such a perfect appearance come into existence by the effort of the peacock himself? Or, could this awe-inspiring colour harmony occur by coincidence? Surely, that is unlikely. Would you believe a friend of yours who tells you that the picture hanging in your room was painted spontaneously, by the accidental splashing of paints? You would certainly not believe him! Therefore, the peacock's tail, incomparably more beautiful than any painting, could not have come into existence by accident. There is no one who would not be astonished by the harmony of colours in a peacock's tail since the One Who creates this perfection is Allah.

A BIRD WHICH MIMICS: THE PARROT

Parrots are colourful birds that live in tropical regions. They lead a very social life. It is really interesting that the parrot shows the generosity of sharing its food with other parrots. In tropical forests, flocks of parrots fly screaming over the treetops. From the answer another flock gives, they find the location of fruit-bearing trees.

Parrots hold their food with their feet and bite it, as if eating a sandwich. Their favourite food is the sunflower seed, which is something we also enjoy. With the help of their curled tongues, they readily divide the seed shell in two–which is a bit troublesome to crack ope –and eat the seed.

They lay two to eight eggs per year. During the incubation period (that is, when the embryos are still in the eggs) male and female parrots sit on the eggs in turn. When the young parrots hatch, they are featherless and feed on the digested foods their parents provide them.

The most important feature of parrots is their ability to imitate sounds. They can pronounce words they hear repeatedly. However, they don't comprehend these words; they only repeat the sounds they hear. They can even imitate a doorbell or the ringing of a telephone. Therefore, if you have a parrot at home, you may frequently assume that the doorbell is ringing.

If these bright coloured, talkative animals had not been created, we could not even imagine that such a creature might exist. That is, we wouldn't even be able to wish that such a colourful bird, which imitates the way we talk, existed. We cannot conceive anything that Allah has not taught us. Allah is the Originator of everything and He creates everything uniquely. This fact is related in the Qur'an as follows:

He is Allah – the Creator, the Maker, the Giver of Form...
(Surat al-Hashr: 24)

As is the case with parrots, Allah creates many beautiful things for us. He shows us His miracles and signs everywhere at every moment. In return for all these, Allah only wants us to recognise the infinite beauties in His creation and be grateful to Him – to thank Him– and to keep ourselves occupied with His remembrance.

DUCKS WITH GREEN HEADS

What first occurs to your mind when one says "to waddle"? Usually: waddling ducklings following their mothers.

Ducks have two techniques they use to feed themselves. While swimming, without plunging underwater, some of them feed on insects and plants. You often see them searching for food, with their head and half of their bodies underwater. Some kinds of ducks, on the other hand, search for food by diving underwater. Their wide webbed feet help them to dive underwater but are not good for walking on land. That is why they only leave the water occasionally, except in the breeding season.

Water fowl such as ducks have air in their bodies. This is one of the reasons they float on the surface of the water. In the duck's body, there exist air sacs that look like tiny balloons. When these sacs are filled with air, they help the duck to float. When the duck wants to dive, it pumps the air out of the sacs and readily dives under the water since less air remains in its body.

These aside, most water fowl are good swimmers. The web between their toes is one of the reasons for this. When they push one foot back, these webs broaden to provide a better pushing force. Of course, it is not a coincidence that all these features required for good swimming exist in water fowl. All these features have been granted water birds by Allah, the Creator of all living beings.

Drakes, the male ducks, always have brighter feathers than female ducks. This is an important protection for the female ducks because they incubate the eggs in their nests, since, thanks to their pale colours, predators cannot see them. Their pale colours being quite suitable for

camouflage, female ducks cannot be seen even at close range. The bright feathers of drakes, on the other hand, attract the predator's attention to them.

When a predator comes close to the nest, the drake takes wing and makes a great deal of noise, making a serious effort to keep the predator away from the nest.

Adult ducks, who stroll in groups, occasionally take care of their babies. Drakes do not incubate. Just a few hours after the ducklings emerge from the eggs, they begin to swim and feed on their own. The newly hatched ducklings know how to feed themselves and to survive, by Allah's inspiration to them.

Think about yourself. What would happen if you were allowed in the water as soon as you were born? Without doubt, as soon as you gulped enough water you would die of suffocation. But, since our Lord has granted ducklings the ability to swim at birth, they don't drown.

Do you know that ducks fly at a speed of 50 kilometres (31 miles) per hour? Do you also know that they avert wild animals by continuously changing their direction? Well, can anyone tell how ducks know to change their direction? Surely, as in the cases of the features Allah granted all other living beings, this is also a feature given to ducks by Allah.

THE BUTTERFLY:
A MIRACLE OF COLOURS

Do you know that butterflies don't have wings when they are born?

That is true! The butterfly is born without wings. It needs to pass through four phases to become the butterfly you see in the countryside or garden. Some have a lifespan of one to two months while some others only live for 24 hours. A butterfly emerges from the egg as a little larva. Soon, it grows into a lovely caterpillar and thus the second phase of the butterfly begins.

There are a total of 14 to 15 rings on a caterpillar's body. It has little

eyes on its head, and a jaw that it uses for chewing. On the front part of its trunk, it has eight legs. When the butterfly is still in the form of a caterpillar, he has no wings and its antenna are very short. Meanwhile, its salivary gland secretes a kind of silk.

A caterpillar does not become longer as it grows; it only puts on weight. Finally, the caterpillar breaks loose from its skin by gradually tearing it. This skin is quickly replaced by a skin more fitting to its fat body. Caterpillars are very delicious creatures for birds that feed on insects. For this reason, our Lord has taught caterpillars various defence techniques. When standing upright, some of them resemble a branch, some of them camouflage themselves by remaining on a leaf that is exactly the same colour as their bodies, while some others play dead. These defence techniques are vital for their survival. They remain alive and grow into butterflies, thanks to these defence techniques.

The caterpillar employs these camouflage techniques also when it grows into a butterfly. Butterflies live in regions that match their own colours. But how do butterflies check that their colour suits the environment since they are unable to see themselves? How can they be sure that they are secure? Certainly, they cannot know or consider any

of these. Allah, their Creator, places butterflies in the most suitable place where they can be secure.

Allah is the "Merciful" and the "Protector", and, as a manifestation of these attributes, He gives many capabilities to living beings, so that they can protect themselves from danger. Otherwise, butterflies are bereft of the wisdom that would make them think that they should protect themselves. Consequently, they themselves could never develop a defence mechanism such as camouflage. The One Who has created all these techniques that make life easy is our Lord, the One Who created the heavens and the earth and everything between them.

The caterpillar, which develops under the protection of the defence techniques given it by Allah, finally reaches the third phase. In this phase, it fills its stomach with as many leaves as possible so that it almost splits apart. In this third phase, the caterpillar imprisons itself in a sack and the metamorphosis begins.

The hard shell that is formed around the caterpillar in this phase is called a "chrysalis". In this shell, it is still and does not eat anything. In this phase, it utilises the energy of the leaves it ate when it was a caterpillar. Chrysalis shells are attached to a leaf, a rock or a branch. If you encounter one of them, have a look at it, because, when you look at the caterpillar inside the chrysalis, you can see the traces of the proboscis and the limbs that will be formed on the butterfly.

After approximately ten days, tearing its

shell open in just a few minutes, the butterfly emerges from the chrysalis.

At that time, the wings of the butterfly have not yet reached their normal size. In the fourth phase, in order to stretch its wings, the butterfly inflates the veins of its wings with its body liquid. When its wings dry, it instantly begins to fly without any training. The wings also help the butterfly in its respiration.

As you see, even a tiny butterfly is a great miracle created by our Lord. Scientists have been conducting research to answer the question: "How does a caterpillar decide to change into a butterfly?" This metamorphosis only occurs because our Lord wills it so. Allah shows us how varied are the creatures He can create, and the unprecedented ways in which He can change them.

Another miracle is that the wings of butterflies are covered with tiny scales. The wings consist of these scales arranged one on top of another. How do you think these wings have come into existence?

Have these scales accidentally come together and formed a wing with its perfect structure?

Have these scales spontaneously united to form a wing?

Has the butterfly himself stuck these scales to one another to form the wing? Did the butterfly himself attach this wing to its back?

A butterfly cannot see its back. But there are perfect symmetrical patterns on its back that it can never see. The scales are arranged in such an orderly manner that the patterns on both wings are exactly the same. If you measure the size of the patterns with a ruler, you will see that they are all equal.

All of these show us our Lord's artistry, eternal knowledge and unlimited power. Upon seeing all these, we should see and reflect upon them and honour our Lord.

INHABITANTS OF THE OCEANS: FISH

The house in which we live, the school we attend, the pavement on which we walk, the parks in which we play, the air we breathe are all things that belong to our world. There are birds, people, trees, plants and animals in this world. However, there also exists another world with which we are not very familiar. We know the existence of this world and sometimes see it on TV. There are also animals and plants that inhabit this world. These animals and plants have no idea about our world. Neither could we live in their world nor is there any chance that they could survive in our world. We could not even breathe one time in that world.

The "other" world we are talking about is the underwater world in which fish live. But, there is

something we need to remember. Fish are not the only living beings inhabiting the underwater world. The underwater world harbours reptiles, insects and plants and shelters millions of kinds of creatures. The creatures living in this world have particular methods of eating, breathing and sleeping peculiar to them.

The respiratory system of fish is different from that of all other creatures. Instead of noses fish have gills. By means of gills, they can use the oxygen in water. The water that is continuously taken into the mouth passes through the gill arches. Meanwhile, capillaries in the gills take in the oxygen dissolved in the water and release the carbon dioxide of the body to the water.

Most fish have nostrils but these are not used for respiration. The nostrils open to tiny sacs by which fish detect the odour of the water that fills these sacs. Sharks, for example, find their prey by means of their odours.

A fish does not have eyelids as do human beings. It looks at the world through a transparent curtain covering its eyes. This curtain resembles a

 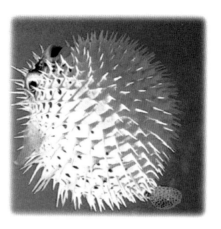

diver's eyeglass. Since they usually need to see objects very close to them, fish's eyes have been created to meet this need. Their eyes are adjusted to see spherical and hard structures close to them. When they want to look at an object at a distance, the lens system is drawn backward by means of a specific muscle mechanism in the eye.

Beside its five basic senses of sight, smell, hearing, touching and taste, the fish also perceives the outside world through its "lateral" lines. Sensitive nerves that lie along these lines perceive the size and direction of objects the fish passes by. In this way blind cavern fish can move very easily in the dark. This system is a kind of underwater radar or "sonar" system.

Furthermore, many fish species have a long and slender balloon-like air-filled sac in the abdominal cavity. They maintain their balance in the water with the help of this sac.

Fish of various kinds created by the will of Allah amaze people with their beautiful colours and movements. You can hardly find such vivid colours as those seen in many fish in any other animal.

You may be familiar with what has been described so far. But, there is another piece of information about fish which will astonish you.

Larger fish usually need tiny cleaner fish to cleanse them of parasites. Sometimes, these cleaner fish readily enter the mouth of a much bigger fish without fear. They clean the teeth and gills of the host fish, a service in return for which the host causes them no harm.

Well, how can the cleaner fish be sure that the big fish will not suddenly swallow it? How does it know that the big fish will not cause it any harm? How can it trust it? It is as if they had an agreement. Let's assume that there exists such an agreement; how could the little fish be sure that the host fish would not violate this agreement and eat it, once it renders its services?

The truth is that the cleaner fish is always vulnerable to its host, but, because Allah has inspired both of them to co-exist, neither does the big fish cause harm to the cleaner fish nor does the little fish feel fear of the larger one. The large fish is cleaned while the little fish feeds on the parasites it cleans. By Allah's inspiration to them, both of them lead their lives in harmony and co-operation.

THE CLOWN FISH

The most interesting characteristic of this fish, which is adorned with brilliant colours, is the place which Allah has chosen for it to live in. The clown fish lives on the branches of a plant-like creature called the "sea peony". There are poisonous capsules on the sea peony's branches and fish touching them are either harmed or killed. However, the clown fish never receives harm from the sea peony. Furthermore, it takes refuge in its branches and protects itself against its predators. A special secretion peculiar to the clown fish protects it against the biting capsules of the sea peony.

Isn't this astonishing? Unlike other fish, this fish secretes a secretion that prevents it from being harmed by the poisonous capsules in the environment in which it lives. And as if it knows that it will not be harmed, at moments of danger it immediately hides itself among these poisonous capsules. How does it know that other fish cannot approach there or that they are unable to secrete such a secretion? No doubt, neither the brain nor the skills of a little fish can grant it such knowledge. There is certainly a power that teaches it all these; this power is Allah, the Creator of the heavens and earth and everything in between.

DOLPHINS WITH SMILING FACES

No other animal is as pleasant and friendly towards human beings as are dolphins. Their docility and friendly manners are obvious from their faces.

During delivery, first the tail, then the body and finally the head of the baby dolphin appear. In order to feed it, the mother dolphin contracts and loosens her milk glands, thereby spraying her milk into its mouth. You can compare this to squeezing a plastic bottle with your hands to spurt out the milk it contains.

Mammals do not need this spraying system to nurse their young. However, such a method is essential in water. Could the mother dolphin herself think up and develop such a system? Could it be possible that she felt the necessity for such a system and supplemented her milk glands with muscles? As you can imagine, this is implausible! As we stressed earlier, Allah created the body of the mother dolphin in a manner that is extraordinarily suitable for the baby dolphin's needs.

The respiratory system of the dolphin is also similar to that of human beings. Yet, unlike human beings, its nostrils are not in the middle of its face but on the top of its head. Like human beings, dolphins, too, inhale air before they dive under water and they retain it in their lungs and then dive. While they rise from deep underwater, just a few metres before they surface, they will breathe this air out forcefully through their blowhole.

You have probably seen on TV how effortlessly dolphins swim in water and even race with ships. They are perfect swimmers. Their smooth slippery skin is the most important reason why they are able to swim so perfectly. These features help them to glide through water and swim very fast. Another feature enabling the dolphin to swim fast is its nose, which is called a snout. A dolphin's snout has the most appropriate shape for fast swimming and has even served as a model for the design of ships. Thanks to this feature, our ships sail faster today than previously.

Do you know that dolphins are bereft of a sense of smell and that they are blind? However, Allah has granted them a very advanced sense of hearing. Dolphins can hear sounds from kilometres away. In addition to that, by means of a system existing in their body that resembles an apparatus used in submarines called "sonar", they can easily find their way and determine their prey's location. This system operates as follows: The sounds produced by the dolphin, which are inaudible to the human ear, spread in the form of underwater sound waves. When these sound waves meet a barrier, they hit it and bounce back. The time taken for the sound to strike a fish or a rock and bounce back shows the distance of the prey or the barrier. This system of dolphins inspired scientists to develop the sonar systems used in submarines.

The dolphin's strong sense of hearing protects it from falling prey to other fish in the ocean.

GIANT WHALES

The biggest inhabitants of the oceans are whales. The whale popularly known as "the blue whale" weighs more than 150000 kilograms (330600 pounds) and is more than 30 metres (1181 inches) long. To have a better grasp of the size of a whale, try to visualise a five-storey building: the blue whale is as long as a five-storey building is tall. Meanwhile, remember that this whale's weight equals the total weight of 25 to 30 elephants.

Well, how does such a giant animal manage to dive down to 800 to 1000 metres (around 39370 inches) in depth and then resurface easily? For example, think of a ship of 150 tons (330600 pounds) and thirty metres (1181 inches) in length. If this ship sank to the bottom of the ocea –that is 1000 metres (39370 inches) in depth–it would take a large-scale operation lasting years to re-float it. However, by the power that Allah has granted it, a whale can rise to the surface in 15 to 20 seconds. Because the bones of the whale are made of a spongy substance filled with oil, the whale can easily remain on the surface of the water.

The whale is also a very skilful diver. Allah has created a body for it that is very resistant to the great pressure in the depths of the ocean. The oxygen circulating in the blood and muscles combines with chemical substances that nourish it underwater or at times it does not breath. It has a circulatory system peculiar to it: it can send blood directly from the internal organs to the brain. This way, until the whale rises to the surface to breathe, it can send the oxygen in its body directly to the brain, the organ that needs oxygen most.

This magnificent system that amazes scientists is a manifestation of Allah's artistry. In this way, the whale can remain under the sea for more than 15 to 20 minutes without breathing.

Moreover, unlike human beings, whales aren't crippled by the bends when they rise very quickly to the surface.

You will probably ask what the bends are. The bends are a sickness that is caused after a rapid reduction in the surrounding pressure. When divers want to dive very deep underwater, they stop at certain points and make their body accustomed to that pressure in order not to be affected by alterations in pressure. This way, they can reach very great depths slowly. But remember that they need to pause and rest at certain intervals during their return to the surface. Otherwise, due to pressure differences, the veins of the diver suffer harm resulting in his death. Whales do not have such a problem, because, Allah has given living beings the features they need to survive in their particular habitats. Whales can live in oceans whereas human beings can live on land.

You probably know that whales spray water from a hole on the top of their head. Do you know that this hole is actually a nose? The whale uses its nose only to breathe. Some people think that the whale only sprays water from this hole. The truth is, the whale releases the air in its lungs. Since this air contains water vapour and is hotter than the air outside, it is perceived as water from a distance.

The body of a whale is usually in the shape of a torpedo and is extremely suitable for swimming in water. While the tails of other fish are perpendicular to the water surface, the tails of whales are horizontal and parallel with the water surface. By means of this tail, the whale pushes itself ahead in the water.

There is a layer of fat approximately 50 centimetres (20 inches) under the skin of whales. The basic function of this layer is to maintain the body temperature at around 34 to 37 degrees Centigrade (93F to 98F).

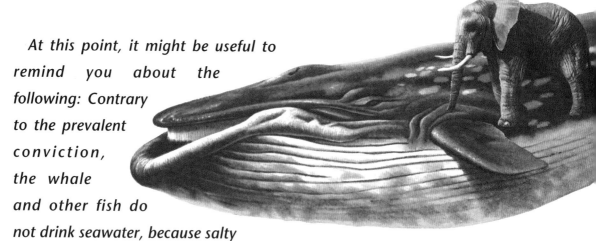

At this point, it might be useful to remind you about the following: Contrary to the prevalent conviction, the whale and other fish do not drink seawater, because salty water is injurious to organisms. For this reason, they meet their need for water from the food they take in.

Each year in December and January, grey whales departing from the North Sea migrate to the southern coasts of Northern America and reach California. Their purpose in migrating to warmer water is to give birth. What is interesting is that the pregnant mother eats nothing throughout this journey; actually, she does not need to. Throughout the long summer days, she feeds in the rich waters of the North, thereby storing more than enough energy for a long journey. As soon as the female whale reaches the coast of west Mexico, she delivers her baby. Baby whales feed on their mothers' milk and store as much fat as possible. This preparation makes them strong enough for migration, which is due to start in March.

Like other mammals, the whale also nurses her babies. But, the babies cannot suck milk since they run the risk of swallowing seawater. As we mentioned before, salty seawater is injurious to whales. Interestingly, as with the dolphin, a muscle surrounds the milk glands of female whales. When the mother whale contracts this muscle, the resultant pressure enables the mother to spray the milk directly into her baby's mouth. This milk is dissimilar to the milk with which we are familiar. It is almost in a solid state and is quite fatty. Thanks to these features, the milk never mixes with the seawater. This substance the baby drinks–in fact, "eats"–dissolves in the stomach. This dissolved food also meets the water needs of the baby whale. As we have seen, Allah has provided baby whales with the most perfect nourishment.

The greasy, transparent secretion covering the eyes of the whale protects it from the harmful effects of the seawater. The whale has a keen sense of touch and hearing. It finds its direction in water by following the echoes of the sounds it makes. The working principle of this sense is similar to that of radar. In fact, this feature of whales has become the inspiration for the development of radar. Scientists believe that these sounds made by the whales constitute a very complex language. This language is important in the interaction and communication among them.

CONCLUSION

Now, let's think about what we have learned so far about animals. From the white ewe that recognises her baby from its odour to the zebra that has a distinctive pattern and symmetry, you have learned many things about animals. However, the most important knowledge this book has provided you is that it is Allah Who has granted all these features to these animals.

As all the examples throughout the book have shown, Allah, the Creator of all living beings on earth, has also taught them how to survive. Sometimes, Allah gives some of this information to the living beings at birth.

For example, while you are reading these lines, you know that you have to keep your eyes open. But for you to see, it does not suffice to know that you need to keep your eyes open. Your eyes have to perform many operations at the same time. You may liken this to a computer game; to start the game, you need only to push the start button, which is a command that starts many complex operations in the computer. Meanwhile, what happens to you is that you sit on your comfortable chair and enjoy the game. Just as a computer could not have come into existence spontaneously, so it is with the components forming the eye. As is the case of all other beings, it is Allah Who has created our eyes and bodies flawlessly.

Our Lord, the Owner of infinite knowledge, has presented you all your physical features at birth, which makes a healthy life possible. That is why, we ought to be grateful to Him for these gifts.

As a person of wisdom learns more about the creation of Allah, his faith in Him becomes deeper and he reveres His might and power more. Actually even a single feature of a creature immediately reminds us of Allah. Not only living beings, but also everything surrounding us and all events that take place provide concrete evidence of Allah's existence. This important fact is stressed in a verse as follows:

In the creation of the heavens and earth, and the alternation of the night and day, and the ships which sail the seas to people's benefit, and the water which Allah sends down from the sky – by which He brings the earth to life when it was dead and scatters about in it creatures of every kind – and the varying direction of the winds, and the clouds subservient between heaven and earth, there are Signs for people who use their intellect. (Surat al-Baqara: 164)

You must also reflect on these facts and never forget the infinite might of Allah, our Lord, and that it is Allah Who gives us all the favours we cherish.

Always keep in mind that all the beauties you see around you exist because Allah creates them.

They said "Glory be to You!

We have no knowledge except

what You have taught us.

You are the All-Knowing,

the All-Wise."

(Qur'an, 2: 32)

Also by Harun Yahya

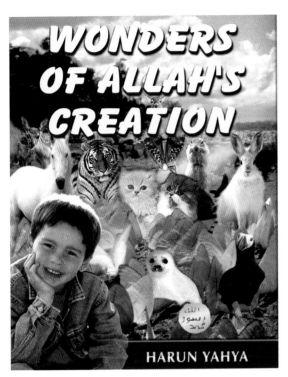

Children!
Have you ever asked yourself questions like these: How did our earth come into existence? How did the moon and sun come into being? Where were you before you were born? How did oceans, trees, animals appear on earth? How do your favourite fruits –bananas, cherries, plums– with all their bright colours and pleasant scents grow in black soil? How does a little tiny bee know how to produce delicious honey? How can it build a honeycomb with such astonishingly regular edges? Who was the first human being? Your mom gave birth to you. Yet the first human being could not have had parents. So, how did he come into existence?" In this book you will find the true answers to these questions.
144 PAGES WITH 282 PICTURES IN COLOUR

Have you ever thought about the vast dimensions of the universe we live in? As you read this book, you will see that our universe and all the living things therein are created in the most perfect way by our Creator, Allah. You will learn that Allah created the sun, the moon, our world, in short, everything in the universe so that we may live in it in the most peaceful and happy way. This children's book is also available in Russian.

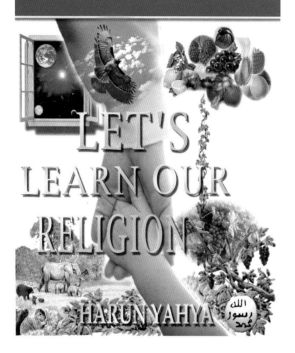

Dear Children!

In this book, we will tell you about the power of Allah, who created your mother, father, friends, all other people, animals, plants, shortly all living things, the Earth, the Sun, the Moon and the entire universe. We will talk about the might and infinite knowledge of our Lord and what He wants us to do and not to do. Do not forget, these are very important matters, which will benefit you greatly!

One of the purposes why the Qur'an was revealed is to summon people to think about creation and its works. When a person examines his own body or any other living thing in nature, the world or the whole universe, in it he sees a great design, art, plan and intelligence. All this is evidence proving Allah's being, unit, and eternal power.

For Men of Understanding was written to make the reader see and realise some of the evidence of creation in nature. Many living miracles are revealed in the book with hundreds of pictures and brief explanations.

288 PAGES WITH 467 PICTURES IN COLOUR

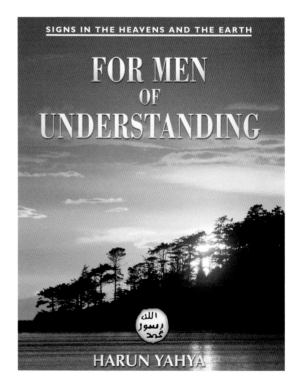

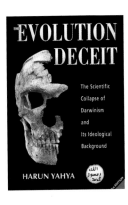

Many people think that Darwin's Theory of Evolution is a proven fact. Contrary to this conventional wisdom, recent developments in science completely disprove the theory. The only reason Darwinism is still foisted on people by means of a worldwide propaganda campaign lies in the ideological aspects of the theory. All secular ideologies and philosophies try to provide a basis for themselves by relying on the theory of evolution.

This book clarifies the scientific collapse of the theory of evolution in a way that is detailed but easy to understand. It reveals the frauds and distortions committed by evolutionists to "prove" evolution. Finally it analyzes the powers and motives that strive to keep this theory alive and make people believe in it.

Anyone who wants to learn about the origin of living things, including mankind, needs to read this book.

238 PAGES WITH 166 PICTURES IN COLOUR

In a body that is made up of atoms, you breathe in air, eat food, and drink liquids that are all composed of atoms. Everything you see is nothing but the result of the collision of electrons of atoms with photons.

In this book, the implausibility of the spontaneous formation of an atom, the building-block of everything, living or non-living, is related and the flawless nature of Allah's creation is demonstrated.

139 PAGES WITH 122 PICTURES IN COLOUR

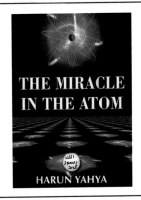

Some of the sayings of the Prophet Mohammed have to do with the signs of the last day. Besides offering information about the signs of the last day, He also gave explanations about the period preceding the last day. In this book, the signs of the last day are examined in the light of the verses and the sayings of the Prophet Mohammed.

164 PAGES WITH 88 PICTURES IN COLOUR

People who are oppressed, who are tortured to death, innocent babies, those who cannot afford even a loaf of bread, who must sleep in tents or even in streets in cold weather, those who are massacred just because they belong to a certain tribe, women, children, and old people who are expelled from their homes because of their religion… Eventually, there is only one solution to the injustice, chaos, terror, massacres, hunger, poverty, and oppression: the morals of the Qur'an.

208 PAGES WITH 276 PICTURES IN COLOUR

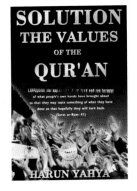

Never plead ignorance of Allah's evident existence, that everything was created by Allah, that everything you own was given to you by Allah for your subsistence, that you will not stay so long in this world, of the reality of death, that the Qur'an is the Book of truth, that you will give account for your deeds, of the voice of your conscience that always invites you to righteousness, of the existence of the hereafter and the day of account, that hell is the eternal home of severe punishment, and of the reality of fate.

112 PAGES WITH 74 PICTURES IN COLOUR

One of the major reasons why people feel a profound sense of attachment to life and cast religion aside is the assumption that life is eternal. Forgetting that death is likely to put an end to this life at any time, man simply believes that he can enjoy a perfect and happy life. Yet he evidently deceives himself. The world is a temporary place specially created by Allah to test man. That is why, it is inherently flawed and far from satisfying man's endless needs and desires. Each and every attraction existing in the world eventually wears out, becomes corrupt, decays and finally disappears. This is the never-changing reality of life.

This book explains this most important essence of life and leads man to ponder the real place to which he belongs, namely the Hereafter.

224 PAGES WITH 144 PICTURES IN COLOUR

Many societies that rebelled against the will of Allah or regarded His messengers as enemies were wiped off the face of the earth completely... All of them were destroyed–some by a volcanic eruption, some by a disastrous flood, and some by a sand storm...

Perished Nations examines these penalties as revealed in the verses of the Quran and in light of archaeological discoveries.

149 PAGES WITH 73 PICTURES IN COLOUR

Darwin said: "If it could be demonstrated that any complex organ existed, which could not possibly have been formed by numerous, successive, slight modifications, my theory would absolutely break down." When you read this book, you will see that Darwin's theory has absolutely broken down, just as he feared it would.

A thorough examination of the feathers of a bird, the sonar system of a bat or the wing structure of a fly reveal amazingly complex designs. And these designs indicate that they are created flawlessly by Allah.

208 PAGES WITH 302 PICTURES IN COLOUR

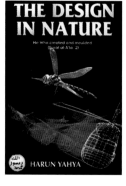

Colours, patterns, spots, even lines of each living being existing in nature have a meaning. For some species, colours serve as a communication tool; for others, they are a warning against enemies. Whatever the case, these colours are essential for the well-being of living beings. An attentive eye would immediately recognise that not only the living beings, but also everything in nature are just as they should be. Furthermore, he would realise that everything is given to the service of man: the comforting blue colour of the sky, the colourful view of flowers, the bright green trees and meadows, the moon and stars illuminating the world in pitch darkness together with innumerable beauties surrounding man...

160 PAGES WITH 215 PICTURES IN COLOUR

In the Qur'an, there is an explicit reference to the "second coming of the Jesus to the world" which is heralded in a hadith. The realisation of some information revealed in the Qur'an about Jesus can only be possible by Jesus' second coming...

Have you ever thought that you were non-existent before you were born and suddenly appeared on Earth? Have you ever thought that the peel of a banana, melon, watermelon or an orange each serve as a quality package preserving the fruit's odour and taste?

Man is a being to which Allah has granted the faculty of thinking. Yet a majority of people fail to employ this faculty as they should... The purpose of this book is to summon people to think in the way they should and to guide them in their efforts to think.

128 PAGES WITH 137 PICTURES IN COLOUR

The evidence of Allah's creation is present everywhere in the universe. A person comes across many of these proofs in the course of his daily life; yet if he does not think deeply, he may wrongly consider them to be trivial details. In fact in every creature there are great mysteries to be pondered.

These millimeter-sized animals that we frequently come across but don't care much about have an excellent ability for organization and specialization that is not to be matched by any other being on earth. These aspects of ants create in one a great admiration for Allah's superior power and unmatched creation.

165 PAGES WITH 104 PICTURES IN COLOUR

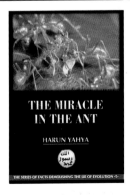

MEDIA PRODUCTS BASED ON THE WORKS OF HARUN YAHYA

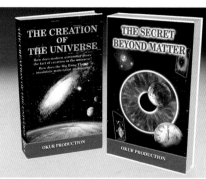

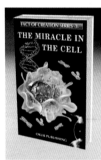

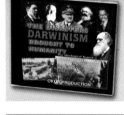

The works of Harun Yahya are also produced in the form of documentary films and audio cassettes. In addition to English, some of these products are also available in English, Arabic, German, French and Russian.